# SAN FRANCISCO MODERN

# SAN FRANCISCO MODERN

Interiors, Architecture & Design

Zahid Sardar | Photographs by J. D. Peterson

Foreword by Mario Botta

CHRONICLE BOOKS
SAN FRANCISCO

*Page 204 constitutes a continuation of the copyright page.*

*Library of Congress Cataloging-in-Publication Data:
Sardar, Zahid
San Francisco Modern : interiors, architecture & design / by Zahid
Sardar; photographs by J.D. Peterson ; foreword by Mario Botta.
p.   cm.   Includes index.
ISBN 0-8118-1965-5 (hc)
1. Architecture, Domestic—California—San Francisco Bay Area.
2. Architecture, Modern—20th century—California—San
Francisco Bay Area.
3. Interior decoration—California—San Francisco Bay Area—
History—20th century.
I. Peterson, J.D. II. Title.
NA7235.C22S356  1998
728'.09794'610904—dc21 98-4137  CIP*

*Designed by Zahid Sardar Design.*

*Printed in Hong Kong.*

*Distributed in Canada by Raincoast Books
8680 Cambie Street, Vancouver, B.C. V6P 6M9*

*10 9 8 7 6 5 4 3 2 1*

*Chronicle Books
85 Second Street
San Francisco, California 94105*

*www.chroniclebooks.com*

FRONTISPIECE  Stanley Abercrombie and
Paul Vieyra's split-level Sonoma home.
RIGHT  Arne Jacobsen chairs at
Adelie Bischoff's Oakland Hills home.
PAGE 6  A glass counter at
Ann Hatch's Telegraph Hill home reveals
artfully displayed jewellery.

ACKNOWLEDGMENTS

In the seven years that I have written about Bay Area architecture and interior design in the pages of the *San Francisco Examiner Sunday Magazine* as well as in many national and international publications, I have discovered that I prefer to write about homes, and particularly about modern homes. Such structures, with their visual clarity, spatial flexibility, and imaginative forms, are frequently designed for individuals interested in the avant-garde. The objects and art collected by these people tell many rich stories; their homes become extensions of themselves, and all their ideas collectively form a vivid word portrait of the people who reflect the vitality of Bay Area life.

I would like to thank all those people who have opened their homes and spoken eloquently about their experience living in them, as well as all the architects, interior designers, furniture designers, and craftspeople who came to me with their ideas.

Many of the homeowners I met have become my friends and have helped immeasurably in constructing this book, some offering advice, even their time and special expertise. I thank all of them, and especially Federico de Vera, Helen Berggruen, Ann Hatch, Norah and Norman Stone, Stanlee Gatti, Stanley Saitowitz, Richard Fernau, Jim Jennings, David Meckel, Daniel Gregory, Lucia Eames, Jim Zack, Marion Brenner, Margery Cantor, Colette Crutcher, Lisa Esherick, Ugo Früh, Sanjay Sakhuja, Dan Friedlander, Ernest Braun, Richard Barnes, and Lucille Tenazas.

At the *Examiner*, I owe William Randolph Hearst III, executive editor Phil Bronstein, my editor Paul Wilner, art director Joey Rigg, and editor Jo Mancuso much gratitude for encouraging my interest in architecture and design.

Editors Margaret Kennedy, Elaine Green and Jody Thompson Kennedy at *House Beautiful*, Marian McEvoy and Kendell Cronstrom at *Elle Decor*, Suzanne Slesin and Lora Zarubin at *House and Garden*, Terry Bissell at *Architectural Digest*, Cathy Lang Ho at *Metropolis*, and Jennifer Wilkinson at *Traditional Home* each have played a special part and I thank them.

I would also like to express my admiration for all those photographers I work with and, in the context of this book, I'd like to thank J. D. Peterson, who has brought his singular vision to the project.

At Chronicle Books, I thank publisher Jack Jensen, for his encouragement. Thanks also to editors Lesley Bruynesteyn and David Featherstone, who meticulously shaped the manuscript; and to art directors Michael Carabetta and Julia Flagg for their good taste.

And without my wife, Tasneem Karimbhai, who listens to the stories when we're on the road to photo shoots and interviews, none of this would be possible.— *Zahid Sardar*

*For my parents and for Tasneem, Benazir & Rizwan*

# CONTENTS

# A NATURAL BALANCE

BY MARIO BOTTA

For me, architecture is the constructed expression of history that reflects the tensions and aspirations of a society.

Any built environment inevitably reflects the quality of life around it. Over time, through buildings we can glimpse the historical conditions, or even the dreams, that formed a particular society.

As the close of this century draws near, any review of its architecture reveals an extraordinary pace of building, one impossible to conceive of in any other time. The pace has been so rapid, fueled by technology and unprecedented engineering, that it has often compromised quality, altering environments so quickly that architecture began to be viewed as an unethical assault on the landscape.

But the best of modern buildings, whose designs have evolved from the tenets of modernism, demonstrate an understanding of what people have always longed for: to live in concert with the cycles of night and day and the passage of the seasons.

Given the speed with which architecture can take shape, the field carries a responsibility for enhancing the natural quality of a place and allowing people the right to healthier lives. Buildings that recognize people's right to live in harmony with nature demonstrate a clear link with it. To assure that a built environment draws benefit from a continuous relationship between the natural elements is a way to find ethical value in the act of construction. To follow modernism means to recognize this as the only context in which to build, and it is a goal that I think all modern architects can share.

In the last decade, there has been a great acceleration in both the complexity and the pace of change in the built environment. Today we have a better understanding of our potential, as well as of our limitations as architects. Buildings have to reflect our new understanding of the balances among the environment, energy use, and society, while they simultaneously draw on avant-garde innovations that characterized the first part of this century. Modernism, tempered with this new knowledge, is very valid today.

It is clear that a single building cannot change an entire city. Through architecture one can, however, consolidate certain ideas, or place oneself in opposition to them. Even a single building is a part of the city. Through the colors and materials selected for the San Francisco Museum of Modern Art, I tried to reintegrate the delicacy of tone and vibration of facade that were properties of the vernacular style in the city at the turn of the century. Today, downtown San Francisco has taken on the look of the International Style that characterizes other new city centers. With the design of the Museum of Modern Art, I intended to add a visual connotation of the city that identifies it as unique, in opposition to the strict "glass-curtain wall" aesthetic. To reestablish the human scale that is evident in the city's neighborhoods through a modern building is, I believe, a way to pay homage to the rich quality of life and the extraordinary light in the San Francisco Bay Area.

FACING PAGE **Fernau & Hartman's Berggruen house.** ABOVE **Mario Botta's SFMoMA.**

# MODERNISM REDUX

Uniquely American, San Francisco was founded as a city of bridges to a mythical European past.

During the late nineteenth century, robber barons built grandiose mansions to echo the overreaching spirit of the 1849 "gold-rush" city that seemingly sprang to life within days. After the devastating 1906 earthquake, a rebuilt City Hall became an homage to the beaux arts, but the disaster itself was more of a trauma than a turning point in the architectural development of the city and the Bay Area region around it. This was in part because Chicago architect Daniel H. Burnham had completed a new plan for San Francisco in 1904 that embodied the precepts of the City Beautiful movement, and it was used to rebuild the city. The Panama-Pacific International Exposition of 1915 presented the face San Francisco wished to show the world—fantastical yet stately—and the romance of Bernard Maybeck's 1915 vaguely Romanesque Palace of Fine Arts, restored in concrete in 1962, is seemingly indelible proof. Drawing more literally from the past, Grace Cathedral, atop Nob Hill, was modeled after Paris's Notre Dame, which was completed in the fourteenth century.

The modern, technological wonders of the Eiffel Tower were not lost on the Paris of the West, however. Willis Polk's 1917 Hallidie Building is credited as the first use of the glass-curtain wall—a radical innovation in an era when walls were supposed to be solid and substantial—several decades before it became the emblem of the twentieth century. No other American architect had gone this far, even though the glass wall had theoretically been possible ever since 1889, when the height-defying latticed Eiffel Tower was engineered. During the 1930s, at the height of the Depression, bridges built using similar technologies spanned San Francisco Bay, inspiring awe and even pride among residents and paving the way for a wider acceptance of modernism in the city. The Golden Gate Bridge and the Bay Bridge remain as enduring symbols of San Francisco's secret, modern, even surreal, heart.

It is interesting to note that the architect who designed the appearance of the Golden Gate Bridge, Irving F. Morrow, was a modernist. He added the faceted plates to the towers' skeletal framework and to the concrete piers at the water level, and he picked the bridge's famously contrary "international orange" color to complement the green and brown of the surrounding hills. In 1933, Morrow designed what may have been the first modern house in San Francisco, for Mr. and Mrs. Henry Cowell, on a hillside in the Forest Hill area, but he found few clients were willing to use full-blown modernist designs. Modernism did not take root as obviously or as swiftly in the Bay Area as it did in other parts of the country.

If one looks at the stylistic elements of most modern buildings in America, the origins of modern architecture lie undoubtedly in Europe. However, the character of the forms and the intentions with which modern elements are used in the Bay Area—the focus of this book—reveal an essentially autonomous architecture in a composite setting, where European contributions are interpreted in an original manner. A brief foray into the history of the European modern tradition; a look at the powerful influence of America's own modern master, Frank Lloyd Wright; and the subsequent assimilation of these seminal contributions with vernacular forms of building in the Bay Area—essentially derived from the gold prospecters' earliest cloth tents, which were gradually insulated with paper and strengthened with wood—will reveal the bias of this book. The examples that are presented within these pages are not intended to be a complete document of all modernist architecture and interior design in the Bay Area, but they represent the wide, eclectic range of Bay Area homes, from Georgian, Victorian, and late Edwardian mansions adapted for modern use to contemporary buildings that have been built in the last few years. The stories and voices of the people who live in these homes and the modernist views of the architects and interior designers who created these spaces will, I hope, put these ideas in living context.

In Europe, fin de siècle excesses had prompted architecture and design critics and artists to lament

FACING PAGE Moderne detailing in heavy steel: The Golden Gate Bridge seen from San Francisco. The building of this and the San Francisco–Oakland Bay Bridge in 1937 gave San Franciscans a first-hand view of modern technology as beautiful.

baroque embellishment. The modernist Viennese architect Adolf Loos, for example, wrote a notorious polemic for a newspaper column in 1908 that equated ornament with crime. In 1924, when Virginia Woolf famously declared that "on or about December 1910, human character changed," she was referring to a show of postimpressionist art in which she saw a portent of great changes to come. New art, architecture, and even literature signaled a rejection of the obsessive historical revivals of the nineteenth century.

In architecture, the term *modernist* is usually equated with the so-called modern movement of the 1920s, sandwiched between two world wars, which found its ideological and stylistic bases in the work of Walter Gropius and Ludwig Mies van der Rohe in Weimar, Germany. Just as the Renaissance is said to have originated in Tuscany because its underlying principles were formulated there by a group of Flo-

rentine artists in the fifteenth century, it can be said that Weimar, Germany, in the 1920s was the birthplace of modernism. The ideas of the Germans, and also of Le Corbusier in France, transformed architecture and design and, in due course, the look of the everyday world around us. These pioneers of modernism made simplicity—what the Japanese call *wabi*, an aesthetic and moral principle advocating austerity—part of their agenda.

By the 1930s, the term *modern* was used to define a twentieth-century style—with roots in the Bauhaus, the design school started in Germany by Gropius—that found fuller expression in the United States. This style was characterized by a simplicity of form with an absence of superfluous ornament, and an emphasis on functional concerns. The word *modern* means recent or current; therefore, it came into use in the discussion and criticism of art, architecture, interiors, and industrial, as well as graphic, design to describe developments of the early twentieth century in which historicism and dependence on traditions were rejected in favor of directions that would relate to the changing social, economic, and technological realities of the machine age.

The work of such pioneering designers as Le Corbusier, Gropius, Mies van der Rohe, and Frank Lloyd Wright is generally viewed as defining modern architecture and design, with its close relationship to modern art of the same periods. Modern architecture—which is characterized by the use of modern materials such as glass, steel, and reinforced concrete and incorporated features such as large glass areas, smooth white wall surfaces, flat roofs, and details using tubular metal columns and glass block—came to be called the *International Style*. Advocates promoted the Bauhaus's ideas of adapting arts and crafts design

methods for efficient, mechanized production and mass consumption.

Architecture such as the work of Wright—which uses traditional and natural materials such as brick, stone, and wood; sloping roofs; and, in some cases, ornament of an original sort—can also be viewed as modern because of its unconventional, assymetrical arrangement of interior spaces that responds to modern lifestyles. Categorizing these developments became problematic, however, because terms such as *modern*, *modernism*, *functionalism*, and *contemporary* referred interchangeably to specific chronological periods, a particular style, or merely a new attitude toward building or designing homes and other structures.

The new rules of architecture and design concerned themselves with even the smallest details—fabric,

furniture, utensils. Under Marcel Breuer, who later lived and worked in the United States, the Bauhaus cabinet shop was one of the first to exploit the possibilities of tubular steel for furniture. Artists such as Gerrit Rietveld frequented the workshops and influenced both teachers and students alike.

The early Bauhaus products shared an emphasis on geometric shapes, such as the furniture Breuer made there in the manner of Rietveld. Although Gropius rejected the idea of a Bauhaus style, the spare and controlled attitude toward form that existed at the school was based on principles of efficiency and economy. The idea that an object or building should function practically and be durable, inexpensive, and "beautiful" spread worldwide within a short span of time.

FACING PAGE Interiors and exteriors of Irving Morrow's Bauhausian Cowell House in San Francisco. Faceted verdigris tiles around the fireplace and other moderne details echo the Golden Gate Bridge. Built-in cabinets and metal-sash windows are distinctive, modernist features. ABOVE Frank Lloyd Wright's low, naturalistic Walker house in Carmel, south of San Francisco.

Advances in technologies surrounding steel and glass that were first discovered in the late nineteenth century led inexorably to the towering "curtain-wall" buildings in every large city today. These were the essential materials of the early modern movement; glass—tested and developed not only for windows but for structures and cladding and walls—became the new futuristic medium. Spare and functional, modern steel-and-glass houses, with their flat roofs, horizontal strip windows, built-in storage units, and bare interiors sparsely furnished with standard wooden and metal furniture, epitomized the ambition of progressive designers in the 1920s to create new forms for a clean, efficient new world through modern technology—"machines for living."

The modernist aesthetic reached maturity in the early 1930s, just when capitalist economies were laid low by the Great Depression, and the rise of totalitarianism in Germany, Italy, and the USSR began to threaten artistic freedom. The roots of the stylistic movement in the United States were established when Gropius and his successor at the German Bauhaus, Mies van der Rohe, immigrated to America and took teaching positions at Harvard University and the Illinois Institute of Technology, respectively. They found an economy based on consumerism (although much weakened by the Depression) and an embracing establishment eager to assume the mantle of cultural leadership. New York replaced Paris as the locus of art; American architecture, based on the European modernist aesthetic, took hold.

The 1932 exhibition *Modern Architecture: International Exhibition* at the Museum of Modern Art in New York, and a book published concurrently—*The International Style: Architecture Since 1922*— popularized the term *International Style* as the label used for the new design and architecture. The exhibition's curators, Henry-Russell Hitchcock and Philip Johnson, defined International Style architecture on the basis of three prominent characteristics: a stress on volume rather than mass, the use of regularity rather than axial symmetry, and the proscription of applied ornament. The exhibition achieved brought European architecture of the 1920s to the forefront of the American architectural debate, undermining the foundations of historicism and the stylistic revivals that had governed American architecture for over half a century.

The International Style came to represent the mainstream of modern architecture through the 1970s. The smoothness and blandness of International modernism—deadened in large part by office towers, mass housing, and government structures—had overtaken cities around the world, becoming an anathema to most people. In response, the modern movement took on new and more-emotional overtones and responded pluralistically in many stylistic directions—such as brutalism, constructivism, futurism, and organicism—until the short-lived spate of postmodernism, whose proponents looked back to classical styles, though for historical memory rather than historical accuracy.

While the open interior spaces designed by Europeans in America such as Walter Gropius and Marcel Breuer tested the tradition of discrete rooms, Frank Lloyd Wright's ideas are considered the principal American contribution to modern architecture. All American postwar architects, and even some Europeans interested in new materials and techniques, were influenced to some degree by Wright's use of them to expand the language of vernacular architecture, as well as by his unique reflections on Japanese architecture and the British arts and crafts movement. Through his design explorations, the value of buildings attuned to specific climatic and site conditions increased and came to be viewed as quintessentially modern. Wright's 1935 masterpiece, Fallingwater, built in Bear Run, Pennsylvania, and a series of modest wartime Usonian homes (a type of low-cost, open-plan, standardized construction he used from 1936 to 1943), demonstrated a softer modernism and suggested a viable American model to architects wishing to be contemporary. A new regard for site, a growing acceptance of historical precedent, and even romanticism became tools to enrich modernism.

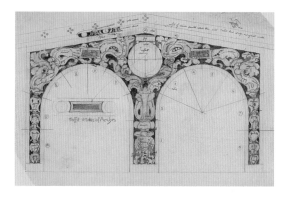

In the San Francisco Bay Area, Willis Polk, Ernest Coxhead, and A. C. Schweinfurth had unwittingly opened the way to such modernism long before it was fully articulated. In the 1890s, these architects were among the first to introduce the West Coast to new, eclectic, nonhistoricist architecture that could be

ABOVE Bernard Maybeck's colored pencil and graphite rendering, *Sgraffito for Lawson House*, Berkeley, circa 1907.

adapted to local building traditions. They evoked historical precedents without slavishly copying them, incorporating traditional moldings, archways, and architectural details from different periods on the facades of their buildings in unexpected combinations.

Bernard Maybeck, another architect from the turn of the century, became the figure with whom Bay Area design was most often identified and who offered latter-day modernists a large body of tradition-based eclectic architecture. Using wood as their favored medium, these San Francisco architects sought to develop buildings that were responsive to the compact, picturesque fabric of San Francisco. Their work reflected the growing popularity of the rustic aspects of the local wood and batten sheds and the landscape in neighboring areas—such as Mill Valley, Sausalito, and Belvedere in Marin County, and Berkeley and Oakland in the East Bay—which were used as weekend retreats. The proximity to the city and the mild, sunny climate of these locations led San Francisco residents to use their simpler cottages as suburban homes throughout the foggy summers, nourishing a taste for rusticity and relaxed patterns of living that have been identified with the Bay Area ever since. When modernism arrived, it was met by this type of healthy regionalism, already rooted in commonsense architecture, which forced it to retreat from the extremes of the mechanistic modern idiom.

Another factor that deflected the strict mandates of European-style modernism was the Depression, which had a disastrous impact on Bay Area architects. Only those who could slide between modernist ideas and sentimental, popular taste could find employment. Successful architects knew how to cross-fertilize

ideas, while architects interested in producing radical International Style designs found small numbers of clients in Northern California. Few banks would lend to borrowers building avant-garde dwellings, which were deemed difficult to resell. The majority of people felt more comfortable in houses designed in a historically recognizable style, or in one that referred to a distant past. These styles continued after World War II, although a regionalized modernism began to make greater inroads than ever before. The inexpensive native style based on good sense and the California wood tradition, rather than on any ideological theories of design, gained increasing currency.

In 1947, the critic Lewis Mumford was the first to identify the flexible architectural tradition of the Bay Area as one that had utilized modernity without succumbing to modernist dogma. Dismissing "High Modernism" as a viable force in the region, he lauded the wood-shingled houses of Maybeck, John Galen Howard, and others who belonged to what he referred to as the first "Bay Region style." Mumford wrote, "That style took root about fifty years ago in Berkeley, California . . . and by now, on the Coast, it is simply taken for granted."

In a 1949 catalog for *The Domestic Architecture of the San Francisco Bay Region*, an exhibition at the San Francisco Museum of Art (now the San Francisco Museum of Modern Art), Mumford reiterated these ideas, marking the contributions of a second wave of Bay Area architects—Irving Gill, Ernest Kump, Gardner Dailey, and William Wurster—who put people and their locality first. Wurster and Dailey, at the time among the most respected of California architects, each contributed essays to the catalog. They

underscored the need for architecture that responds to the long dry season with large, informal open spaces achieved by eliminating wasted space—long halls and stairs.

Wurster and Dailey's ideas tied into the practical, utilitarian tenets of Bauhausian as well as Wrightian philosophies. They both used elements of the International Style in their commercial and residential buildings but softened them for the Northern California context, evoking historical vernacular precedents rather than a future assured by the machine. "It is a truly popular architecture," Wurster wrote of the Northern California house, celebrating houses that brought feeling to function. This style of building came to symbolize what is now called the second "Bay Region style"—the often low, horizontal single volumes broken by a measured grid of doors and windows, with overhanging sloped roofs inspired by Japanese structures—which was described by East Coast critics as a kind of soft modernism.

Unlike Wurster, Dailey bandied with versions of the machine-age streamline moderne, varying his work in the 1940s between modern and moderne. A series of San Francisco apartment houses at the foot of Coit Tower (itself a moderne landmark on Telegraph Hill), including one for himself, are examples of Dailey's formal, elegant moderne designs. In the hillside 1939 Owens House in Sausalito, Dailey (associated with Joseph Esherick) showcased the structure of the building by opening up the two principal two-story facades with glass.

Wurster more prominently demonstrated the argument that functionalism had metamorphosed from an abstract machine aesthetic to a form more

solutely necessary. Instead of classical, monumental houses, he built boxy, larger-than-expected volumes to create luminous living spaces. Pointing to Wurster's lasting legacy, Mark Treib, a professor of architecture at the University of California, Berkeley, wrote: "If today Wurster's architecture appears so ordinary or invisible, it just may be because his lessons . . . have been so completely absorbed into the currents of home building."

Standardized and prefabricated housing became a burning issue in the years after American entry into World War II, when burgeoning military bases on the West Coast required immediate housing. Scarcity of conventional materials forced the exploration of materials that previously had been passed over. Glass products replaced metal, scarce during the war; plywood and particle fiber boards were available for consumption instead of wood. Advances in polymer chemistry gave rise to new synthetic fibers and families of plastic materials. Nylon, for example, developed for parachutes, replaced silk in upholstery. Wartime structures were made with modular panel systems that incorporated the new material of plywood as its principal element in conjunction with reinforced concrete block; laminated-wood-and-steel frames were used in addition to standard wood frames.

Such avant-garde ideas altered the formal aspects of the rectilinear International Style, allowing an increased use of organic forms in architecture that derives inspiration from Wright and from the explorations of another visionary architect, R. Buckminister Fuller, the pragmatic engineering aesthete and in-

humane and appealing to the lay audience. From the late 1920s until he died in 1973, Wurster built simple, woodsy, unadorned buildings whose beauty depended on proportion, scale, and an honesty of materials. One architectural commentator compared Wurster's shacklike Northern California buildings to those built by "a carpenter endowed with good taste."

Even though Wurster didn't exactly create new dwelling forms, his ability to hide the hand of the architect behind seemingly uncomplicated buildings designed for daily use set him apart from his peers. His 1927 solution for Sadie Gregory's farmhouse in the Santa Cruz mountains—a low L-shaped batten-covered fair-weather house with an enclosed courtyard and—is considered a seminal Wurster design. It launched his prolific career and became a precursor of the "ranch house" that continued as the single most influential California building form.

The source for Wurster's designs was often the commonplace: painted wood and stucco over wood-frame colonial or Victorian building types. He modified these with the angular restraint of modernism and the International Style, and added his own ethos of simplicity—no beam or post was larger than ab-

ABOVE William Wurster's Clark Beach House, Aptos; interior view of his Gregory Farmhouse, Santa Cruz. FACING PAGE A. Quincy Jones and Frederick Emmons's 1956 model Eichler homes.

ventor of the geodesic dome. It is interesting to note that after the war, Ray and Charles Eames—the giants of American industrial design—used fiberglass, a glass-reinforced plastic designed for aircraft radar domes, and plastic resin materials from war-surplus stores, to manufacture their molded fiberglass-shell armchair, which is now a design classic. This chair, distributed through Herman Miller, achieved the goal of producing low-cost, mass-produced, high-quality furniture, and it has become ubiquitous in modern interiors today.

The formal lessons—standardizing and prefabricating housing—learned by West Coast architects during the war, were also used in the postwar years to build low-cost, attractive tract housing. Many Japanese-influenced features of Wurster's buildings—the glazed/screened central porch, the direct connection of indoors and outdoors, the linked kitchen-dining-living room, and balanced lighting such as skylights in kitchens, to cut glare—were praised in the pages of popular home magazines and found translation in many tract homes by private builders. Wurster's contemporaries, Donn Emmons and his brother Frederick, had developed a modern model—minimal front fenestration, open rear plan, entry court, and projecting garage—that anticipated later residential designs such as the influential subdivision houses done for the Palo Alto developer Joseph Eichler in the late 1940s. Many of these were designed by either A. Quincy Jones, of Los Angeles, or by Robert Anshen, of the Bay Area.

Many young architects who viewed San Francisco as the center for innovative domestic design from 1937 to 1942, among them John Ekin Dinwiddie and

Harvey Parke Clark, took up and continued the Bay Region tradition. In the 1940s, they were joined by a younger contingent of Bay Region architects that included John Funk, Clarence W. Mayhew, Ernest Born, Mario Corbett, Francis Joseph McCarthy, Henry Hill, Michael Goodman, and Vernon DeMars, all of whom built houses in the Bay Area. Joseph Esherick, a Gardner Dailey protégé, went on in the postwar years to become a teacher, dean of the architecture school at the University of California, Berkeley, and a major voice in the last phase of the Bay Region tradition. Several projects included in this book are influenced by his ideas.

After 1945 and particularly in the 1950s during the occupation of postwar Japan, there was a widespread interest in Japanese culture in the United States. Japanese architecture influenced the modern movement everywhere, but most obviously in areas such as California, where there were large concentrations of people of Japanese descent. The lightness, elegance, minimalism, and rectilinear geometric forms of Japanese architecture were readily applied over vast, unbuilt tracts. Flexible interior partitions, lanterns, and decorative pottery reflected a Japanese aesthetic, as did the intimate relationship between exterior and interior. In the informality of those postwar years, journals such as *House Beautiful* objected to Le Corbusier's celebrated dictum that a house is essentially a machine for living and turned instead to the intangible properties of warmth that houses of traditional form might offer. Decorative accessories—banished from interiors by high-modern purists—were reintroduced by interior designers, a move welcomed in California and elsewhere as refreshing.

Lifestyle magazines instructed future homemakers on how to live in the spirit of the times; rather than seeking a particular style of house, owners ought to plan a rational house. A modern kitchen should not be small, but should be a "living kitchen," such as those seen in Bay Area homes. Californian modernism, which had come to imply ease, comfort, and gracious living, symbolized the popular acceptance of modernism in the United States.

There was a backlash from the bastions of early modernism, of course. In 1948, Alfred H. Barr Jr., director of collections at the Museum of Modern Art in New York, somewhat derisively called the Northern California style of understated building, which had been emulated abroad and echoed in British, Swiss, and Scandinavian magazines, "the International Cottage Style." When Henry-Russell Hitchcock and Arthur Drexler mounted an exhibition of American architecture at the Museum of Modern Art in 1952, they deemed the Bay Region tradition no longer significant.

By the early sixties, it seemed, the Bay Region tradition had indeed run its course, until two key figures, Joseph Esherick and Charles Moore, brought it new vitality. In Esherick's hands, the Bay Region style includes structures with redwood or shingle siding, often capped with shed roofs with no overhangs; sometimes he uses stucco (as in the Napier house, included in this book). At Sea Ranch, a development on five thousand windswept oceanfront acres formerly used as sheep pastures in Sonoma County that was planned by landscape architect Lawrence Halprin, Esherick and Moore executed designs that are heirs to Frank Lloyd Wright's essays in ecological and environmentally responsible designs. In 1965, the first seven houses and a lodge built at Sea Ranch were Esherick's shed-roof structures, developed not arbitrarily but from an examination of the wind-bent profiles of hedgerows.

ABOVE Sea Ranch, located a hundred miles north of San Francisco, is a 1960s utopia that spawned a renewed interest in rusticity.

Set low in the landscape, these sod-covered redwood "earthhouses" are architectural windbreaks. For the well-known ten-unit condominium, Moore fashioned a series of shed-roof vertical rectangles out of which protruded a wild array of bays, interspersed with awkwardly placed windows that claimed the site in a naturalistic, craggy way. Moore's structures became a rough, crude vernacular assertion, a composition of vertical spaces divided not by floors but by vertically connected platforms. Although Sea Ranch was a utopian ideal intended for unique surroundings, what followed this seminal project matured in the 1980s as a renewed interest in things regional, and in regionalism as an ecological and ethical stance.

In 1991, a fierce brushfire destroyed hundreds of homes in the Oakland Hills, erasing architectural treasures that were decades old, including some by Maybeck, and fueling much debate about the appropriate way to rebuild in the region. Serendipitously, in November that same year, an exhibition opened at the San Francisco Museum of Modern Art titled *In the Spirit of Modernism*. It examined the work of four Bay Area architectural firms: James Shay, Tanner Leddy Maytum Stacy, Jim Jennings Arkitecture, and William Stout Architect. In that show, Stout and Jennings, industrial-style Miesians at heart, and the environmentally conscious Shay and TLMS posit what seem like two ends of the rebuilding argument, each advocating the use of technological advances in the spirit of modernism.

However, modern houses reviewed for this book—especially those built in the Bay Area during the boom of the mid-1990s to late 1990s—reveal no clear formal consensus about one or the other approach to building. What appears instead is a simultaneous embrace of both industrial-style and ecologically conscious ideas. Modernism, in San Francisco, may have become the Bay International Style.

In the Bay Area, modernism has come full circle formally, moving from the regional umbrella of vernacular wood houses such as those by Fernau & Hartman, to recognizably modern, even Bauhausian buildings. Recent examples include Corbusierian homes by South African Stanley Saitowitz, a Miesian structure (sprayed with concrete over foam resembling adobe) by New York emigrés Paul Vieyra and Stanley Abercrombie, as well as houses by New York–based postmodernist Robert Stern and Los Angeles deconstructivist Frank Israel. With eclectic stylistic nuances, other Bay Area architects such as Robert Swatt produce contemporary interpretations of 1930s International Style buildings merged with distinctly Japanese conceits. However, despite their classic modernist forms, these new buildings incorporate environmental lessons learned from Wright, Wurster, Moore, and Esherick.

Some new Bay International Style buildings, several remodeled homes, and interiors by Bay Area designers such as Federico de Vera, Gary Hutton, and Craig Steely are grouped here to highlight these overlapping design philosophies. Whether they are indoor/outdoor homes, galleries for personal collections (Eamesian "functional decoration"), rehabilitated open-plan Miesian warehouses, modern rooms within historicist buildings, or Bauhausian cast-concrete cubes or biomorphic shapes that recall the poetry of Le Corbusier's chapel at Ronchamp, they are tempered with a concern for the environment.

Some of the examples included in these pages evoke the outdoors metaphorically; gardenless, Saitowitz's Bischoff residence is conceived as a living and working space in a U-shape plan around a sunken living room, an echo of the inner garden of courtyard houses. Eric Haesloop creates a promontory-like space to enjoy the view from a client's San Francisco high-rise pied-à-terre. Others, such as Scott Johnson, a one-time student of Esherick's, use exterior rough-sawn cedar and flagstone indoors, blurring the lines between inside and out.

Eschewing the strict all-white dictum of traditional modernists everywhere, Bay Area modernists play comfortably with a vibrant color palette. Interior designer Richard Brayton and artist Mardi Burnham's city home is one striking example. Architect Richard Fernau and lawyer Sarah Cunniff's Berkeley home is another. For radiologist Dan Siedler's remodeled craftsman-style home, Daren Joy has used a "shielding" material, copper, for walls.

In a courtyard-style house for two art dealers in Reno, architect Mark Mack employs ideas he first used in the Bay Area: double-sided indoor/outdoor fireplaces, colors inspired by the surroundings, and a Loosian floorplan. Mack calls this his "most California house," demonstrating how well the flexible Bay Area model travels to other parts of the country.

In the end, although these extraordinary Bay Area homes seem to have eavesdropped on every conversation about modernism, even sliding to tangential thoughts in a rambling sort of way that presents no one formal language, they still think and talk in the direction of what is important—landscape, climate, and comfort.

# HOME AS GALLERY

# HATCH RESIDENCE
## A HOUSE ON TELEGRAPH HILL

Judging by the portrait at the top of the stairway leading to Ann Hatch's sunny San Francisco living room, her mother was a brooding woman, while Hatch, who was barely twelve when Salvador Dalí painted the pair, was already breaking free from her family's hold.

Although she comes from a long line of art collectors (her great-grandfather, T. B. Walker, founded the Walker Art Center in Minneapolis), Hatch chose not to build a formal art collection, but to concentrate instead on creating the Capp Street Project, a not-for-profit gallery and resource for emerging installation artists. In the same breakaway spirit, she bought two adjacent Edwardian houses on Telegraph Hill and asked architect Stanley Saitowitz and interior designer Federico de Vera to convert them into sleek, modern, light-filled spaces.

Saitowitz, noted for a modernist style of building, and de Vera, owner of three San Francisco stores specializing in avant-garde art objects, approached the joining and remodeling of Hatch's houses as they would conceive an art installation: Both the internal stairwell and the ground floor double as galleries, while vitrines, glass-topped tables, and other glass, wood, and steel items were designed as display cases elsewhere in the house. Hatch was determined to save the original facades, so a new awning and metal gates are the only clues to the changes within. Just inside the entryway, however, industrial steps, in an open grid-work pattern, have replaced the old staircase.

Inconsistencies in floor and ceiling heights between the two buildings presented a problem for the architects, but Hatch's enthusiasm for vivid color proved invaluable to its resolution. "The spaces had to

FACING PAGE At the head of the metal stairs is a 1960 portrait of Ann Hatch and her mother by Salvador Dalí. The sleek living room, with B & B sofas from Limn and custom designs by Federico de Vera, has an expansive view of the bay. ABOVE An adjacent living space is reserved for heirlooms and artwork mixed in with simple mementos. A wood, glass, and aluminum display case by de Vera holds a terra-cotta vase by Picasso. Artfully arranged firewood—spoofing Martha Stewart—is an ongoing installation project by Paul Discoe. A metal sculpture nearby is by Tom Marioni. RIGHT The metal awning outside Hatch's joined buildings.

be interwoven and we did that with color," Saitowitz says. From the third-floor landing you can see—like points on a compass—green in Hatch's bedroom, a deep-blue wall just past her son Tim's bedroom, and Pompeiian red walls in her office. The dining room, with its huge, retractable skylights, is painted a light-absorbing greenish blue; and where the ceilings of the two living rooms meet awkwardly, Saitowitz used a wall of lemon yellow to separate them.

When de Vera became involved, midway through the reconstruction, he was faced with a palette of disparate colors and an eccentric collection of French antiques, modern art, and mementos from Hatch's

FACING PAGE The red armchair is by Poltrona Frau; table by de Vera. ABOVE & RIGHT In the dining room, heirloom china from the Walker family inspired artist Timothy Wells's trompe l'oeil drawer. The artwork on the wall is by Isamu Noguchi.

previous homes. He started by diverting some things to storage, but he also found inspiration in many of her treasures. The Asian motifs in the dining room rug he designed are a nod to her heirloom Chinese porcelains. To complement a Raphael Soyer canvas of nudes in the living room that had belonged to her mother, de Vera bid at auction for a similar Soyer of clothed figures that now hangs in the bedroom.

"Ann's furniture wasn't exactly my style," de Vera admits. To unify Louis XVI or Biedermeier pieces with his own creations—such as occasional tables of glass and anodized aluminum tubing—de Vera relied on a color strategy similar to Saitowitz's. Chairs from different periods were recovered in bright colors, and in the dining room, blue velvet seats cleverly harmonize the mismatched chairs Hatch accumulated over the years. The shade of blue was determined when de Vera saw a matched set of antique blue-and-gold china from Hatch's maiden aunt.

De Vera's skill at juxtaposing diverse objects is evident in the living room as well. In a long wood-and-glass case set on slender steel legs of anodized tubing, a vase by Picasso is harmoniously displayed next to valuable jades and plastic souvenirs. Even a

coffee table of metal and glass is a display case; through its transparent top you can see works by Gay Outlaw, a book by William Saroyan, and even a paper fan showing a topless drag queen. Perhaps the most serendipitous decision was de Vera's insistence on converting the first floor into a game room and a gallery, where such keepsakes as Tim's baby shoes and a dog bone in honor of Hatch's pet, Elmo, sit beside more exalted items. "We didn't want people to think us too precious," Hatch says, laughing. "It's a fun house. I've lived here for some time, and it is only just revealing itself."

CLOCKWISE FROM LEFT The first two stories of Hatch's house are finished with an acrylic terrazzo floor by artist Bill Maxwell that is imbedded with mother-of-pearl, glass, and metal to resemble water with ripples; windows at the base of the new stairwell leak in light, while sunlight cascades through open gridwork designed by Stanley Saitowitz. The industrial materials—painted steel and galvanized treads—are echoed in a suspended video installation by Alan Rath; A floor milled from Presidio lumber forms the bedroom landing; a blue wall brightens the way to Tim Hatch's room.

Greens and blues tie Hatch's bedroom and bathroom to an aquatic theme. Eighteenth-century allegorical ivory figurines representing the seasons are placed above her bed, a floating raft by de Vera. A Raphael Soyer canvas of clothed figures, which de Vera acquired at auction, complements nudes by Soyer in the living room. A silver leaf chair is visible in the dressing room.

## STONE RESIDENCE
### A HOUSE IN PACIFIC HEIGHTS

Norah and her psychologist husband Norman Stone's Pacific Heights home hosts a sizable collection of art within its twelve-thousand-square-foot space. Their Georgian revival mansion, designed in 1927 by Arthur Brown (the architect of City Hall), has become a foil for the Stones' extraordinary collection of pop and contemporary art. "We love this house—it's perfect for our collection," Norah says.

ABOVE A Jeff Koons bouquet of painted wood sits on a stand intended for real flowers. LEFT Deco chairs flank a 1976 group of ten canvases by Andy Warhol titled *Skulls*. FACING PAGE Gallery yellow on the living room walls sets off an untitled piece by Richard Prince hung above an antique chest of drawers. "It's an American altarpiece—a 1968 Camaro car hood resting on a panel covered with Bondo," says Norman. On the far wall is a Lawrence Weiner drawing titled *A Rock Smoothed to a Stone*. In the foreground, a 1968 mica-and-wood piece by Robert Smithson called *Site Non-Site, Portland Mica* sits on the floor.

A ROCK SMOOTHED TO A STONE BY THE

Like many early modernists, the couple discovered modernism through art.

The previous home the Stones owned was decorated in a pronounced art-deco style that competed with the art they began to collect ten years ago. When Thomas Bartlett, their interior designer, recommended a Tuscan color palette to correspond to the Palace of Fine Arts, which studs their 180-degree view of the bay, they demurred. "We needed a gallery setting," says Norah.

In the end, the decorative moldings of the grand house were toned down with a color just a shade lighter than the subtle yellow walls, and the sofas (most of which are below eye level) were covered with pale, richly textured fabrics. Several rooms—Norman's library, a card room, and an upstairs gallery—were preserved in the style of Frances Elkins, who designed the interiors for the house's previous owners, the Zellerbachs, during the 1930s. "We were lucky because we bought a period house," Norah says. "Nobody had redone the bathrooms and their wonderful 1930s fixtures. We preserved as much as we could." The dressing room off the master bedroom, detailed with silver-leaf walls and Lalique crystal tiles, was saved; the hand-painted wallpaper in the entry hallway was restored; and a hand-tooled bar and bar stools, along with other original pieces, were retrieved at the Zellerbach estate auction.

FACING PAGE Saving many of the original Frances Elkins furniture from the 1930s, Thomas Bartlett designed an interior for the Stones that is deliberately understated to highlight their art collection. RIGHT A 1990 Sigmar Polke acrylic-and-artificial-resin-on-fabric painting, titled *Five of Hearts*, is suspended from the library ceiling; the hand-painted wallpaper in the hallway was restored.

I went to see a psychia

Despite the obvious splendors of the mansion, it is the modern conceptual art that holds sway, and the juxtaposition of the artworks' surreal, ambiguous, often disturbing messages and the elegance of the interiors is startling. The deeper you go into the four-story house, the more complex and explicit the artists' messages get. Works by Lawrence Weiner, Andy Warhol, and Jeff Koons are in the living room; another Warhol in the dining room; Robert Gober and Eva Hesse in an upstairs gallery; Sarah Lucas and Richard Prince in the bedroom.

Both Norah and Norman studied art and photography, and they meet regularly with the art consultant who guides them. "A lot of what we've learned about modern art has come through our connection with the museum," says Norman, who is a trustee at the San Francisco Museum of Modern Art. "But because I am a community psychologist, I gravitate toward contemporary art that refers to the problems of contemporary society. It pushes us emotionally and intellectually." The work frequently makes references to AIDS, sexual identity, and gender issues. In particular, the couple avidly collects unsettling mixed-media video installations by Matthew Barney.

"When I met Norman, he was more introverted," Norah teases. "He used to collect tribal masks."

ABOVE A startling red-and-black Warhol in the bone-colored dining room is a recent acquisition. LEFT A 1991 video presentation and installation by Matthew Barney in the basement yields its meaning after several viewings. Its inscrutable title, *Anabol (A) Pace Car for the Hubris Pill,* doesn't tell you that Barney uses the displayed apparatus—an exercise mat, surgical instruments, a plastic sucrose capsule, a thermal gel pack, and a pearl—to enact a sexual metamorphosis depicted in the video. FACING PAGE In the bedroom, the psychologist hangs a 1989 Richard Prince work titled *Tell Me Everything;* its silk-screened words on an acrylic background are designed to fade over the years. Original dressing rooms seen through the doorway in the master bedroom and on the first floor echo the mansion's resplendent past. Handmade floors, mirrored walls, and silver-leaf details throw the art collection into sharper focus. "Art can shock you, but it has to be more. It has to go somewhere," says Norman.

## FRANKLIN RESIDENCE
### A HOUSE IN PACIFIC HEIGHTS

In the 1970s, modern architecture was not what people looked for in San Francisco. "Luckily, it was our taste," says Ruth Franklin, referring to the simple house she and her husband, Marc, acquired when they moved from Portola Valley to the city. The couple, avid collectors of African and Oceanic art, were originally from New York and moved to teach and work at Stanford.

Their three-story house was designed by the noted San Francisco modernist William Wurster and his associates at Wurster, Bernardi, and Emmons. "For Easterners, the name Wurster wasn't known. Ted Bernardi was still practicing and we met him," she says.

From blueprints in Bernardi's possession, the Franklins discovered that their home had been remodeled once for the original owners by the very architects who built it. While that pedigree meant little to them, they admired the house's fenced-in courtyard with an understated gated entry, its simple wood-clad exterior, its three bedrooms, and its comfortable, large-size rooms with expansive white walls and high ceilings to display their burgeoning collection of tribal art. Since modernism had fallen so out of favor at the time, they were also able to admire the low price tag.

Their home seems like a carefully orchestrated design, filled faithfully with 1950s and 1960s furniture to complement the elegant, clean-lined spaces within each room, but, according to Ruth, that was not the case. "We were married in 1958 when Danish modern was the rage," she says. They bought most of

ABOVE From the private entry courtyard, at the middle level of the Franklins' three-story hillside house, its resemblance to suburban Eichler houses from the 1950s and 1960s is obvious. LEFT Wrought-iron "people" chairs by John Riley near the red front door offer a clue to the owners' passion: votive sculpture from Africa and Pacific Island art. FACING PAGE Janus figures and other African masks and sculpture are displayed in an acrylic case that the Franklins discovered in a store going out of business.

their Scandinavian furniture, including an Eero Saarinen suite of table and chairs for the kitchen, shortly after the wedding; the rest—a 1960s dining table and other pieces—was gathered slowly, one at a time. The couple insists that their major design preoccupation was never architecture or interior design; when they moved to the West Coast, it was, and still is, African and Oceanic art.

But such art, the Franklins know, has important lessons to teach. Just as building blocks used in kindergarten shaped the ideas of Le Corbusier, Mies van der Rohe, and Gropius, the simple, geometric forms of the primitive art being discovered in

Africa during the early twentieth century influenced Western art and architecture, bringing a new vocabulary of simplified, powerful forms. For the Franklins, newlyweds who were both interested in modern art, a specific encounter in 1959 became a turning point in understanding these connections. One evening while living in New York City, where Ruth worked at the journalism school and Marc taught law at Columbia University, the couple went on a charity art tour. "We went to see Jackson Pollocks . . . they were many and large, but what we noticed in a corner was something we had never seen before—a New Hebrides fern figure. We had no idea what it was," says Ruth. Their fascination drew them to attend classes on the subject (Columbia was one of few places teaching anything about such tribal art) and that eventually led them to acquire their first pieces.

"It was called primitive art in the 1960s. It wasn't even regionalized then," says Ruth, now a curator at the Stanford University Museum of Art concentrating on Africa, Oceania, and the Americas. "In Europe, the museums of ethnography are still asking whether this art should be shown in the Louvre," says Marc. Even Picasso evidently claimed he had not heard of African art early in his career!

"We have come to appreciate the patina of use more," says Marc, referring to the tendency of the French dealers to have the pieces cleaned before sale. "Nowadays, collectors joke about the French patina," says Ruth. The very first figure the Franklins bought, a Songye votive sculpture from the eastern part of Zaire, was stripped clean. "I look at it now and it looks raw," she says.

Today, the Franklins' collection, shown publicly in 1988 at the M. H. de Young Museum in an exhibition called *Forms & Figures: Dynamics of African Figurative Sculpture*, is probably one of the most personal American collections of such art. Skillfully distributed and arranged in every room of the house, it exceeds three hundred objects. "In the past twenty years, we've had over a thousand pieces pass through our hands," says Ruth.

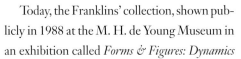

LEFT In the living room, Norwegian modern furniture from the 1950s complements the handmade simplicity of stylized African and Oceanic sculpture. RIGHT Unusual anthropomorphic chairs from the 1960s are by Pierre Poulin. FACING PAGE Built-in shelves and a horizontal band of windows with shutters to modulate the light are subtle Wurster details.

Some of those pieces are from serious excavations in Africa that were undertaken only after World War II. "There was fabulous metal work as well as terra-cotta and stone work, but our collection is principally of wood," says Marc. "Our first [wooden] Songye suggests we have not progressed very far," he adds jokingly.

RIGHT The Franklins' Danish modern furniture from the late 1950s—a Saarinen suite of table and chairs for the kitchen, a dining table—and other pieces were gathered through what Marc Franklin calls "slow accretion." ABOVE The large mask hanging on the wall in the dining room, was originally used ritually. Although the Franklins and other collectors view tribal figure sculptures, masks, and votive instruments as art, "they were all made for rituals in their places of cultural origin," says Ruth. FACING PAGE The 1960s-style bedroom has an original corner fireplace; doors open to the courtyard.

# BOYD RESIDENCE

## A HOUSE IN THE OAKLAND HILLS

There's a madness that overtakes some collectors, an urge to fill every corner with objects that represent a specific theme or an era. Recognizing this propensity, Michael and Gabrielle Boyd, young, passionate collectors of twentieth-century art and furniture, chose to exercise restraint and instill a modernist order in the renovation of their Oakland Hills home.

RIGHT In the living room, a fireplace of cinder blocks is a Frank Lloyd Wright influence. BELOW The stools are by Wright. The red, yellow, and black wall sculpture is by Donald Judd. Michael Boyd, also a recording composer and musician, collects unusual guitars. Seen here, a steel guitar and percussion instruments. FACING PAGE Looking toward the bay view, a chaise by Le Corbusier, Pierre Jeanneret, and Charlotte Perriand; surfboard table by Charles Eames.

wooden plank-and-rail furniture. Another find were the wooden chairs Marcel Breuer made at the Bauhaus when he was twenty.

The Boyds knew that they wanted to highlight this important collection, but not in a sterile white showcase. In Daren Joy, a partner in the San Francisco architecture firm North American Stijl Life—named after the Dutch modernist design movement and because of Joy's taste in arranging rooms as tableaux and still lifes—the owners found, literally and figuratively, a twin sensibility. Joy's twin brother, Daven, and his partner, Travers Ebling, both owners of Park Furniture, also joined the design team.

The renovation for the Boyds' small, L-shaped house surrounding a gravel garden involved gutting this 1950s Eichler-style original, with its boxy rooms and low beamed ceilings, and reconstructing it over Daren's new Mondrianesque floor plan, which eliminated hallways while linking volumes of space that empty one into the next. The addition of a second-

Icons of midcentury furniture by Frank Lloyd Wright, Charles and Ray Eames, and Gerrit Rietveld, as well as relatively recent pieces by Frank Gehry or Donald Judd, make theirs a textbook collection. Bauhaus, de Stijl, surrealist, and dada pieces are a companion interest. The art is mostly from the post–World War II era, and the furniture is twentieth-century avant-garde. "In a very narrow area, we are experts," says Michael, who has cross-referenced every piece they own in books on the subject. "There aren't any holes in the furniture collection." In that sense, the furniture itself is a library.

"When we are at the Met or at MoMA, we think we are in our own living room," says Gabrielle. In some cases, the Boyds have even found seminal prototypes of designs that were meant for mass manufacture, such as Rietveld's de Stijl standard, the Red/Blue chair that was inspired by Wright's simple

ABOVE Upstairs, a Charles and Ray Eames bookshelf divides a seating area from the bedroom; in the distance, a plywood-clad wall with a square opening allows views both of the study, where the couple displays prized prototypes, and of the bay.
RIGHT The sitting area is a showcase for chairs by Frank Gehry, an Isamu Noguchi coffee table, an Eames folding screen, and a couch by Alvar Aalto. Metal mesh doors to the closets are by Dennis Ludemann. FACING PAGE The dresser is by Park Furniture.

story study, master bedroom, and their own bathroom gave the couple ample space to dovetail spaces for their collection, as well as room for floor-to-ceiling libraries and rooms for their two boys.

Another device used to enlarge the space visually was to remove most of the walls and reinstall them as partitions with see-through openings. For instance, standing in the new kitchen, with its chunky, aluminum and stained-wood, industrial-style aesthetic, you can look through glass-backed wood cabinets into the dining room and at the view of the Golden Gate Bridge beyond it. A new flight of stairs with aluminum risers and wood treads leads up to the bedroom and an adjacent study overlooking the bay; a wall that divides the rooms is sheathed in precisely mitered maple plywood and pierced with a square window to frame the bay view and a glimpse of the bridge, visible from the couple's bed. The new rooms evoke the midcentury era in which most of their collection was made. The overall impression is one of rigorous simplicity, but the spaces are lavished with subtle, finely machined details: a pattern of screws in a bureau of nickel-plated steel; aluminum edging on every door; ebony-stained floors that flawlessly meet crisp white walls. The new furniture by Daven Joy and Travers Ebling is designed to complement the interior as well as the collection. Using steel, mahogany, aluminum, neoprene, and even perforated sheet-metal doors, the Park Furniture team echoed Daren Joy's interior architecture. To the owners' delight, some pieces created here for the first time have become staples in Park's line of simple, straight-lined modernist furniture. "The nice thing is," says Joy, "Michael's collection is never finished."

FACING PAGE In the see-through wood-and-glass kitchen cabinets built into the wall, the Boyds display an eclectic collection of industrial design from the 1930s and subsequent eras. Perforated-back wood chairs are by Frank Lloyd Wright. In the background, a black door pockets into a plywood-clad wall to reveal a streamlined wash basin. ABOVE In the first floor library, prototype bookcases by Park Furniture; walnut stool by Charles Eames.

# OLIVER RESIDENCE

## A HOUSE ON TELEGRAPH HILL

For years, Steve and Nancy Oliver, art collectors and patrons of contemporary art and architecture, have considered San Francisco home; they maintained a pied-à-terre there for twenty-seven years while they lived and raised a family in Orinda.

When it was time to change the location of their primary residence for better access to urban delights such as the ballet and theater, their city dwelling on Telegraph Hill had to be replaced by one that could accommodate visiting children, grandchildren, and an art collection that had not been fully displayed or enjoyed in their previous Cape Cod–inspired house.

They knew from their living arrangement in Orinda, as well as from their experience with San Francisco architect Jim Jennings, a die-hard modernist, that modern art would find hospitable surroundings in a contemporary building.

FACING PAGE The front elevation frames interior views at night, shielding the more private areas such as a study/sitting room at the very top. THIS PAGE The Olivers' home, below, comfortably mixes practicality with a kind of rigorous asymmetry. A glass-enclosed balcony floats above the entryway, overlooking the courtyard; squared horizontal and vertical planes offset the building's cylindrical heart, which resembles Coit Tower, top right. The central concrete cylinder contains stairs, bridges, and a red leather–lined elevator, middle right, that connect the wings as well as the different levels. The entrance leads directly into the cylinder; a black-walnut shelf by Cheri Fraser complements Christian Boltanski's *Les Bougies*, an artwork with candles and metal. The bridge leads to the living room. A sculpted figure by Manuel Neri stands near the garage entrance, bottom right.

Jennings and Oliver, who owns a construction firm, had known each other since their school days, and they had worked together on many buildings, including the Olivers' weekend ranch house in the wine country. The Olivers were so familiar with Jennings's aesthetic that they knew where his explorations of the generous—by city standards—but nonetheless hemmed-in site on Telegraph Hill might lead.

The ambitious building the Olivers asked Jennings to design had to fit within the small envelope of the original—a nondescript shingled structure—which stood obtrusively between neighboring back gardens. In response to the Olivers' desire for living spaces, galleries, a guest suite for relatives and visiting artists, and a rental apartment, Jennings designed a sculptural, magnificently articulated metaphor for urban living.

"The design relates to buildings with bay windows [a Bay Area norm] and to the urban spaces surrounding this building," says Jennings.

The four-level building is conceived quite simply as two wood-frame and stucco rectilinear forms fitted neatly against a fifty-foot-high, seismically reinforced, poured-concrete cylindrical core. "There is a suggestion of focus and axis, but these are not symmetrical," Jennings says. Bay windows, a glass-enclosed balcony, decks, and other variations of height and fenestration modulate the two wings of the house,

LEFT A bridge of sandblasted glass connects the living room to the dining and kitchen spaces. Above the fireplace is Rick Arnitz's 1991 *Taps*. FACING PAGE Gary Hutton's interior scheme for the house is deliberately subdued to emphasize the art collection, rotated twice a year. His furniture is designed low, upholstered in pale, richly textured fabrics, and arranged in informal groupings. His tub chairs, and chairs by Mirak in the foreground, are spirited accents.

echoing houses in the neighborhood, while the soaring cylinder that anchors them represents the city itself. The architect has laid out his "streets"—the stairs, bridges, and an elevator that connect the wings as well as the different levels—through this central structure. An enormous skylight—reinforced to serve as a viewing deck—caps the cylinder, flooding it with light that leaks down to the entryway; although the bridges cutting across the cylinder are made of steel with perforated anodized aluminum side panels, their glass plank floors render them weightless visually.

"There are several levels of privacy," says Nancy. The first floor has two guest bedrooms above the five-car carousel underground garage; the living and dining rooms and the kitchen are on the second; the master bedroom and a study are on the third. Ceiling heights are deliberately lowered at each level, creating increasingly private spaces: the lofty, three-story entry vault, the seventeen-foot-high living room, a seven-and-a-half-foot, low-ceilinged study at the top.

Interior designer Gary Hutton, who has worked with Jennings before, created a palette of subtle monochromatic contrasts to emphasize the Olivers' rotating art collection. Throughout the house, white gallery-style walls balance the warmth of maple floors and the opalescent coolness of the concrete; in the living room, organized in informal, asymmetrical groupings, understated low tables, deep tub chairs, and sofas upholstered with richly textured but pale fabrics—all Hutton originals—follow the same rationale.

The structure's unusual reversed siting—at odds with zoning regulations that require houses to be built at the front of city lots—caused many delays, but there were unforeseen advantages. "Time helped the

design . . . it wasn't the kind of building that evolved from a single idea," says Jennings.

To ensure that the new building could be built exactly where the old one stood at the rear end of the lot, "we needed fourteen variances," Steve recalls. In the end, the several-years-long battle was worth fighting he says, because "we got to keep our south garden."

"Contemporary houses with contemporary gardens are overkill," says Nancy, who loves gardens where a sense of tradition prevails. To suit her taste, the planted beds are interspersed with walkways cobbled with stones from the old Lombard Street hill. The garden is now an elegant entry court, planted discreetly to emphasize a sense of procession—from country to city—by landscapers Delaney, Cochran and Castillo.

Moving to the city was a kind of site reversal for Nancy as well, requiring many adjustments and variances. "It was like starting over for me," she says, concerned about living within what she had feared might be too strict a shell without any curvilinear forms. But once again, there were unexpected dividends. In Orinda, the couple had to get into the car just to get a carton of milk, while their city neighborhood's tight parking conditions force a different, healthier approach. "Here, you have to walk," says Oliver.

ABOVE The window by Jennings's tower reflects a view of Coit Tower. A cantilevered concrete stair leads up to the steel-reinforced, glass-plank deck that doubles as a skylight to cap the cylinder RIGHT In the bedroom, near a door that opens to a terrace, is a 1990 Martin Kippenberger work on paper. FACING PAGE The study/sitting room at the top has a view of Fisherman's Wharf.

# STREMMEL RESIDENCE
## A HOUSE IN RENO, NEVADA

The versatile, modern courtyard house, popular in the San Francisco Bay Area and all over California, permits such ease of living, indoors and out, that it is being exported, adapted for varied topographies, to places with similar though less moderate climate conditions.

The nine-acre arid site where Peter and Turkey Stremmel live seems nothing more than undisturbed brush, scattered rocks, and scurrying quail, a desert wilderness that their architect, Mark Mack, describes as so fragile, "it would take ten years for any of this to grow back . . . if at all." Still, the site proved to be a suitable location to build a California courtyard house.

When the Stremmels, owners of a thriving art gallery, showed the Austrian-born, previously San Francisco–based, architect their five-thousand-foot-high site with a view of downtown Reno, hills, and snow-capped peaks, the introduction culminated in a polychromatic building of cubes and trellises that rises magnificently like modernist sculpture.

"It is my most California house," the architect is fond of saying. The Stremmels' house demonstrates the wide-ranging applications for the designs Mack first developed in the Bay Area. Indeed, the mostly one-story, seven-thousand-square-foot structure opens freely on all sides, creating breezeways to make the most of hot weather, expanding Mack's ongoing dialogue with California-type environments. His houses invariably emphasize the relationship between indoors and out with open, loftlike floor plans that epitomize modern Californian architecture. These same features are also prominent in the Stremmels' western Nevada house.

"The outside becomes something like Lanai and Hawaii during the summer," says Stremmel, "when we eat by the pool. It is an amazing transformation after a long and brutal winter." Winter is spent hours at a time

LEFT A terra-cotta wall in the living room supports the library loft; beneath Jean Dubuffet's painting *La Coiffeuse* is a moderne wood-and-metal, stone-topped chest by Terry Hunziker. ABOVE Peter and Turkey Stremmel's house gets its cues from the California courtyard house, where trellises—painted steel, in this instance—define or shelter outdoor rooms. Colors express functions: the red cube is the living area; the yellow holds guest quarters. FACING PAGE Simple shapes of cinder block (notice the indoor/outdoor fireplace), stucco, steel, and concrete make complex juxtapositions. The upholstered furniture and mahogany and oak tables by Seattle-based designer Terry Hunziker; dining chairs by Vicente Wolf.

ABOVE A pivoting front door under the guest wing. LEFT A reflecting pool marks the built-up boundary. BELOW Exterior cinder-block walls continue indoors below the guest wing and library. FACING PAGE In the dining area, an informal ceiling of galvanized corrugated sheeting and a constellation of suspended lights evoke the outdoors.

in an upstairs library, one of two spaces on the second level.

Mack originally sketched a large shedlike roof (inspired by the open corrugated shelters seen along the endless Nevada highways) under which he organized playful, colored blocks to serve his clients' wish for a spacious living/dining area with large wall surfaces to display modern artworks and equally expansive windows to take in the view; three bedrooms for themselves and their daughter; a large kitchen; a den that would flow to a walled pool court; and guest facilities.

What ensued, however, was more attuned to the conditions of the site. To engineer a protective solid canopy that could also withstand the 130-mile-per-hour winds that sometimes lash the hill proved too daunting. Instead, what Mack developed is part

ABOVE In the guest powder room, Mack delights in modernist, functional details and combines wood, concrete, and glass artfully. FACING PAGE In the master bedroom, a vanity chair by Gerrit Rietveld. Reflected in the mirror is a landscape by Wolf Kahn.

aluminum roof, part trellis, and part breezeway hovering overhead, interconnecting the various enclosed and courtyard spaces. Also, in order to build at the sloping site at all, it was necessary to form a plinth that could also be used to stack building supplies. "I carved half of it out of the slope and elevated the other half so that the house would float over the site," Mack says. "If people had overrun the site willy-nilly, it would have ruined it for years. Truck tracks can't be erased. Sagebrush and delicate flowers would disappear." Bay Area landscape architect Peter Walker helped to site the house, and the entire plinth became the boundary of the house, a metaphor for the first grid laid on Western soil. The shielded side of the structure is the domestic side, with the lap pool and backyard, while the living rooms facing east look onto the view of the city. Beyond the boundary of the house, nature takes over. It might have been "more appropriate technology" to build an adobe house like the one the Stremmel's had before, "but they are very expensive and lack flexibility," says Mack. "Here, an art dealer needed high spaces … he almost wished to live in a gallery."

The balloon-frame structure that he created with commercial-style windows was "domesticated" with color. Walls of integral plaster, and floors of concrete with radiant heating, are site-appropriate and energy-efficient notes. Just as Mack placed indoor-style lighting and an open fireplace outside to enhance the idea of outdoor rooms, he introduced exterior materials such as cinder block into the interior. In the dining room, the corrugated roof is exposed to view.

With interior designer Terry Hunziker, the owners worked out a palette of muted colors to tame the vast twenty-four-foot-high walls in the larger rooms and, in effect, to harmonize with the rich rust and crimson hues of the desert. "We also wanted a neutral backdrop for our modern art," says Stremmel. Hunziker designed several original pieces of furniture inspired by the work of Jean-Michel Frank, one of the Stremmels' favorite designers.

"The right side of the building is a guest house that is separated in function, and you walk through it to get to the main house," says Mack. This "gateway" makes for a processional entry into the house that is a series of open and enclosed spaces. Stremmel says that within a year after he moved in, they used all of the house. "Not just a few rooms, but every square inch."

"In a sense, this house is a culmination of ideas I have nursed through other houses," says Mack proudly. "Here, you can see them clearly. In the site and the program, I had no constraint."

# WALKER/KIMPTON RETREAT
## A HOUSE IN THE WINE COUNTRY

"People use their gardens more than views," says architect Sandy Walker, who with his wife, Kay Kimpton, found a small, one-acre garden with prune and plum trees right off the Silverado Trail near St. Helena. They quickly added cypresses and English laurels and a lawn on the west side. Views of the neighboring vineyard become extensions of their pastoral hideout. "We wanted to see as much of that as possible," says Walker.

They knew from experience, though, that a wine country rural aesthetic would never work for them, being die-hard urbanites connected to the art scene in

FACING PAGE In the living room, a lithograph from the series *Back to Black*, by Richard Serra, hangs above the fireplace. An Eames lounge chair, an Eileen Gray chrome-and-glass side table, and Le Corbusier Michelin chairs are all modern notes for the interior, which was deliberately left spare to highlight a rotating art collection. ABOVE The steel and glass entry. RIGHT The dining table of laminated wood with showy corkscrew legs was made by Robert Croutier. The Dakota Jackson dining chairs were originally designed for the San Francisco Main Library.

LEFT A poolside loggia beyond the dining room can be closed off by garage doors set on vertical tracks. TOP Large wicker chairs by Ralph Lauren double as lightweight, easy-to-move outdoor furniture. ABOVE Views of vineyards from every level make the house seem expansive. FACING PAGE, ABOVE Walker's sculptural spiral stairway. FACING PAGE, BELOW In the library, where Walker spends most of his time during weekends, is a classic fauteuil by Eileen Gray.

San Francisco. Kimpton is a contemporary art dealer, while Walker has some far-reaching connections with art—his great-grandfather, T. B. Walker, founded the Walker Art Center in Minneapolis, and his brother, Brooks Walker Jr., is on the board of trustees at the San Francisco Museum of Modern Art.

To suit their urban tastes, they built a barnlike modernist building that is a hybrid of many styles. "I gave serious consideration to the Villa Savoye [Walker's favorite building] as a model…some day I'll build it," says the architect. As a starting point, Walker drew inspiration from a house architect Adolf Loos designed for the family of philosopher Ludwig Wittgenstein. "It's a cubist house—they all had flat roofs—with tall metal doors, shiny floors, dark sash, and deep-set windows," says Walker. "I tried to prove the point that a modern house can have a pitched roof."

But in the end, the form stemmed from what they wanted. Their "minimalist Tuscan farmhouse" is raised several feet above ground, not in homage to Le Corbusier's famous Villa, but to look over the vines next door. The dull metal roof was an alternative to hard-to-maintain clay tiles, and the large steel frame and the glass doors and windows are standard modern building elements. Stucco on the exterior resists fire.

"Galvanized corrugated material would have been too shiny, but I also didn't want to do a traditional Mediterranean building," says Walker.

The thick, double-framed walls insulate against the extremes of temperature the wine country sometimes experiences, and a stucco finish gives the sense of heavy masonry. New trellises of unfinished lumber along the east wall will offer cooling shade when covered in vines. Stained concrete floors sealed with epoxy

throughout the first floor flow seamlessly toward the pool and tennis courts on one side of the garden; a loggia room that acts as a buffer between the living spaces and the pool can be closed off in winter and on cool evenings by pulling down a set of garage doors on vertical tracks. "This also means we never have to put away any of the outdoor furniture," says Kimpton.

Between doors to the kitchen and the library, a metal spiral staircase painted white like the wall is placed dramatically, like sculpture, facing very tall steel-and-glass front doors that rise to a two-story height. As you go up the stairs toward the bedrooms on the second floor, new perspectives of the valley become visible. "There's a long view toward the vineyards and a short view through the loggia toward the pool," says Walker. The master bedroom has an open wall that looks down into an atrium space "so that we can converse from floor to floor," he adds. From there one can see a two-story-high "art wall" and also catch glimpses of the pool.

Large, white wall spaces and an open floor plan accommodate Walker's collection of classic modernist furniture as well as Kimpton's art, which includes Serra, Warhol, and less well-known artists such as Wesley Kimler, whom she represents.

"We wanted minimal but comfortable furnishings in keeping with the spare detailing of the house," says Kimpton. In the living room, a banquette built around the fireplace provides a lot of seating in addition to Walker's favorite Michelin and Barcelona chairs.

"I sometimes feel in some way that this house is more formal than our city house. It doesn't have old beams and quirky details, but it is more focused on our needs," says Walker.

SMALL SPACES, BIG IDEAS

# FRIEDLANDER COMPOUND

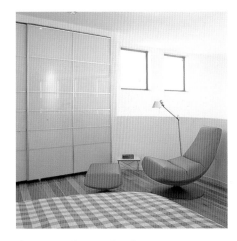

The South-of-Market Area, or SOMA, in San Francisco is an area redolent with the city's past as a thriving port. This is where goods were shipped to or from—by rail or boat—and the brick or steel-and-concrete industrial-style structures that housed the wares still dot the section, little changed with time. But these days, the old buildings are more likely home to graphic design studios and software companies. In one such warehouse, diagonally opposite the train station, Dan Friedlander, a principal in Guthrie-Friedlander Architects and a furniture designer, set up Limn, a store selling modern furniture and furnishings that became a colorful institution in the evolving neighborhood.

"I had always dreamed of building my own house," says Friedlander, and when a piece of land next to his leased store became available he had the opportunity to do just that. "It was the last piece of railroad spur that was left in this location." For a long time, the wedge-shaped lot remained as a thoroughfare for pedestrians and provided informal parking for the store. "It was thought basically impossible to build on this property; it had a long driveway without space to turn around," Friedlander remembers, but the lot soon became his.

FACING PAGE An oil-on-canvas dog painting by Chinese artist Zhou Chunya titled *Helgen Is Running*, hangs on the terra-cotta stairwell wall. Just near the entryway to the kitchen, Eames dining chairs surround a glass-top dining table from Cassina. "If you furnish to scale, a small room can seem large," says Friedlander. The oil painting in this dining area, *Billy King's Dad*, is by Billy King. ABOVE In the curved bedroom loft overlooking the living room, closet doors are like foldaway screens; wood floors add warmth. An Eames wire table and Tolmeo floor lamp by Artemide are grouped with a contemporary lounge chair covered in rust-colored leather. RIGHT Through the open gate door, a view of the central courtyard.

With Richard Foster, an architect who had worked with Skidmore Owings and Merrill for nearly twenty-five years and who was then in Friedlander's employ, several designs took shape. "We made two separate town houses at first, and we even tried something more conventional," says Friedlander. He ultimately decided, after innumerable visits to the planning department, to build a mixed-use live/work complex that would be innovative without disturbing the visual fabric of the area.

The building is extremely simple. It is essentially a set of four-story boxes modulated by nine rows of windows, twisted to face south and also to fit against the property lines in a U-shaped plan; the boxes are connected at the first floor by a single-story gallery space that opens to an entry courtyard.

The goal was to find pleasing interior and exterior juxtapositions while providing privacy for each of the twin town houses (they do not share common walls). "Most live/work lofts do not provide sufficient privacy. They are too open," Friedlander says. Within twenty-four hundred square feet of space, the architects have ingeniously dovetailed four bedrooms and two bathrooms with doors that shut. "There are lots of places to hide. Even if the rooms are small, different activities can go on in private," observes Friedlander. His wife, Kazuyo, has an office at the very top. "Several times we didn't know we were each at home," he says.

FACING PAGE More classics, an Eames lounge chair and ottoman, and a stool, are limited editions from Herman Miller. *Swimmers*, an oil-on-board painting, is by Yanik Wagner. RIGHT "I don't like everything to match," says Friedlander, so he experiments with textures and shapes, using tiles from Ann Sacks in all the bathrooms.

ABOVE, LEFT A stair tower of galvanized metal mesh leads up to Friedlander's living areas on the top three levels of the building. ABOVE, RIGHT A long, pebbled walkway leads to the entry gate. BELOW The courtyard is surrounded by a gallery space and public kitchen for large parties. Sculptural red-painted steel stairs to a model unit and a canvas canopy make it a showy setting. FACING PAGE In the living room, Friedlander displays a prize from his collection of Memphis furniture, a bar and sideboard by Italian designer Masimo Iosa Ghini. Another, a seat by R. Mranzi, rests by the window wall. "Frog" chairs of woven plastic over chrome frames and B & B's "happy hour" push-back sofa are paired with a classic Noguchi walnut and glass-top coffee table.

Using color in integral plaster walls and stains for the concrete floors covering radiant heating systems, the architects have set off the stairwell as a freestanding sculptural tower within the space. The master bedrooms in both units are curved bays overlooking the sixteen-foot-high living spaces. Two-foot-square windows perforate the exterior walls from floor to ceiling, affording urban views from every level. For all its dramatic moments, the interior is simply finished with minimal detailing, except in the bathroom, where Friedlander experimented with different textures and tile shapes.

Outside, stairs leading from the courtyard to each unit have also been conceived as sculpture. "We wanted to make the courtyard exciting, since it is a very public space," says Friedlander. "We could have had just one stairway, but this way each side feels equally private and individual." The asymmetrical stairway designs—one an overturned serrated-steel box painted red, and the other, to Friedlander's apartment, made of galvanized metal mesh that will be covered in vines over time—give the courtyard visual punch.

Exterior stucco finishes custom-mixed by San Francisco–based colorist James Goodman echo the interior walls, but the palette is tertiary, subdued to blend in with neighboring warehouses. "Taupe seemed strong but not risky," says Friedlander. "Instead of color, we played with patterns."

Looking at the house from the street corner—eighty-eight feet away—it is hard to imagine that the building wasn't always there, but what makes one look again is the crisp formality of the boxes and the unusual fenestration that confounds perspective. From that distance, the building looks like a nine-story high-rise in the middle of downtown.

## CLARK/SMITH KITCHEN
### A KITCHEN IN THE RICHMOND DISTRICT

Bruce Tomb and John Randolph, partners in Interim Office of Architecture (IOOA), a San Francisco–based industrial design and architecture think tank, adhere to many aspects of Bay Area modernism and aim for designs well integrated with the site while mixing various craft and structural traditions for avant-garde, yet extremely functional, spaces. Most of their projects have been small renovations, of residences and lofts for artists such as graphic designer Tom Bonauro and photographer Larry Sultan, that allow unconventional solutions. Their own live/work spaces are currently being constructed within the old police station in San Francisco's Mission District, an example of 1930s institutional architecture that usurped the no-nonsense functional vocabulary of streamlined modernism as its own.

One IOOA project, a kitchen design in a Richmond District flat in San Francisco, exemplifies the characteristics and inventiveness of Bay Area modernism and bears inclusion here. When the owners, Elaine Smith and Jeff Clark, hired the pair to transform their small, standard-issue 1970s-style kitchen into something special, they didn't foresee that it would lead to a hybrid of Shaker-like simplicity, Zen ritualism, and machined, Bauhausian modernism. "We are always reinventing," says Tomb. "Part of what we do is critique. We ask questions; we take things apart. Sometimes that leads to new things, and sometimes we discover things are good the way they are." Tomb has worked closely with experimental artists such as David Ireland, conducting architectural renovations as though they were archaeological investigations. Not surprisingly, at their own police station live/work spaces, Tomb and Randolph have opted to retain the jail cells, fitted with new skylights, as living spaces.

Clark describes an early meeting with the designers: "They talked of a concept of *subtraction* rather than addition." Ripping out a wall between the pantry and kitchen was the first step. After removing the wall cabinetry and matching Formica counters, the architects also eliminated a light-obstructing greenhouse that had been installed outside the old sash windows. In opening the north wall behind the old kitchen cabinets, they discovered several plastered-over rectangular openings, ventilation holes

TOP In the dining room, San Francisco Bay Area originals: *Scissor* dining table designed by Bruce Tomb and John Randolph; chairs by Thomas Jameson; cast aluminum vase by Eric Blasen. In the kitchen, a niche contains a television set behind glass. LEFT Under the counter, steel-and-aluminum shelves give the built-in cabinets a crafted look. A "California Cooler" window revealed, restored, and glassed-over lets in light. FACING PAGE The architects combined a pantry and kitchen by eliminating a wall and restaining the disparate wood floors a cherry red; a silver-gray ceiling and pale yellow walls complement a cast-cement yellow counter by Buddy Rhodes. The custom chandeliers of electrical conduit, junction boxes, and blown-glass shades are by IOOA. A wedge-shaped kitchen table of counter height was built to butt against a vegetable sink and work-top to double as counter space. Storage cabinets are fitted with handles to match those of a Sub-Zero refrigerator opposite the table.

for once-standard but now outdated cool-storage cupboards called "California Coolers." These holes, revealed, restored, and covered with glass, bring extra light into the now-elongated kitchen and establish a new "geography" for the room. "A lot of thinking went into bringing the light in; we even bounced exterior lighting off the neighbor's wall to bring light back in," says Tomb. "It's a Japanese idea," adds Randolph.

The once-dark room feels roomier than its 180 square feet. The original pantry windows and mismatched hardwood floors (now stained a uniform cherry red) in the two rooms were left in place at the owners' request, giving the designers another predetermined condition to work around. "Instead of feeling obliged to repair with wood the scar on the floor where the old cabinets were, we felt we could use glass tile instead," says Tomb. The floor tile wrapped upward becomes a backsplash that sticks out a few inches from the wall to accommodate new water and drainage pipes, creating a convenient low shelf for small objects to rest on.

The new kitchen shows off its systems, revealing what's normally concealed; washing, cooking, and storage areas are clearly defined by sculptural furniture and fittings. Different materials—cement for counters, hand-finished maple (a Shaker staple) for cabinetry, brushed steel and aluminum for shelving, custom electrical conduit and blown-glass for chandeliers—enhance the functions the furnishings are intended for. For example, the stove is next to black-slate counters and backsplash; artist Buddy Rhodes's sunny yellow, cast-concrete counters bounce back light near the windows; a deep-gray cement vegetable sink adds a sense of earth below fresh greens; and glass mosaic tile is used near the washing area. Faucets used in hospitals for the kitchen sink, and chrome foot pedals for the vegetable sink, allow both washing and sanitation.

To make the long room seem wider, the designers eliminated the upper kitchen cabinets on one side. At one end of the galley, above an appliance garage hidden in the wall, a frosted-glass cabinet conceals a small television set. The galley kitchen counter tapers off into a wedge-shaped maple table wide enough to spread the morning paper, blurring the line between work and repose: The true contemporary San Francisco kitchen is also a living space.

LEFT Glass floor tile replacing the old cabinets also covers a "wet" wall that forms the backsplash. Framed photographs by J. D. Peterson. A wrist-blade faucet over the sink, and a faucet with foot pedals for the vegetable basin, keep hands free. FACING PAGE A breakfast nook.

## ANDERSON RESIDENCE
AN APARTMENT ON RUSSIAN HILL

In 1962, the Alexander Hamilton Hotel, one of the first all steel and concrete hotel towers in San Francisco, became the city's first condominium conversion. The twenty-one-story complex not far from Union Square was designed in 1929 by architect Albert Herman Larsen, a Northern California native who started his career in association with the firm Weeks & Day, architects for the Sir Francis Drake and the Mark Hopkins hotels. The faded environs of the previously luxurious hotel abut the Tenderloin District, but it is experiencing a revival

LEFT A ribbed-glass screen creates a visual barrier while letting light in from the kitchen window. RIGHT, TOP, AND BELOW Anderson has avoided some of the icons of modernism: Eames, Le Corbusier, Aalto. In the living room, he placed a Frank Gehry seat for its shape; but for comfort, a sofa from a vintage store fits the bill. Prints from the 1930s are by George Platt Lynes; the color Polaroid is by David Leventhal. FACING PAGE Book boxes of wood and metal by Park Furniture in the vestibule. In the kitchen, working with the original stove, Anderson reconfigured ungainly storage within a new maple-veneer wall divider with a pass-through counter; three colored prints are by Todd Hido.

PHRENOLOGY
BY
L.N.FOWLER.

LARRY CLARK 1992

BEATON

JAN DIBBETS · Interior Light

ANDREAS FEININGER

DENNIS HOPPER

DENNIS HOPPER

ROBERT MAPPLETHORPE

GEORGE PLATT LYNES

MAPPLETHORPE ALT...

MAPPLETH

model

Duane Michals

Photograph

HITLER MOV

James Danziger

70

LOLA ÁLVAREZ BRAVO

EL LISSITZKY

because of its relative proximity to San Francisco's new Museum of Modern Art and other arts complexes in the Yerba Buena area.

Like that of many steel-frame structures built after the 1925 Paris *Exposition Internationale des Arts Décoratifs et Industriales Modernes*, the Hamilton's exterior is art-deco moderne, reflecting the prevailing ocean-liner elegance of the day, its rigorous concrete punctuated with geometric detail, foliate forms, and Egyptian-inspired shallow pilasters. Inside, however, the apartments had few details to match the exterior.

When interior designer Richard Anderson (of Candra Scott & Associates) moved into one of the condos, he found it remarkably unchanged, trimmed plainly with seven-decade-old wood around doors and windows and finished with carpeting laid directly over the all-concrete floor.

"It was a great space, and I liked the layout," says Anderson. Small and surprisingly low-ceilinged for a deco building, the apartment contained a living room and a dining room separated from the single bedroom by a bathroom, a walk-through closet, and a kitchen. The sprawling urban views from the eighteenth floor, a saving grace, expanded the meager 850 square feet visually.

Rooted in the 1920s and 1930s, the building's design represented one of Anderson's favorite periods; the other being the clean-lined International Style of 1950s modernism. As a leitmotif that would allow him to explore both these sympathetic vocabularies, Anderson chose to tilt the apartment's interior to the latter style, with less ornament but also with an eye

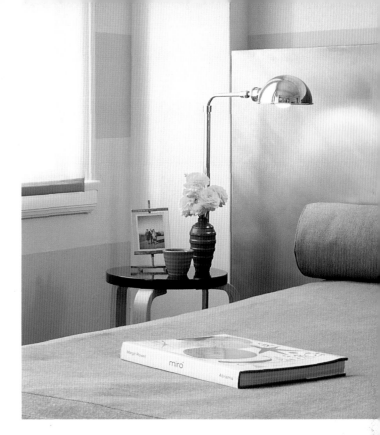

toward eclectic innovation. "I didn't want a historic document," he says, resisting any urge to slavishly recreate a design era that has fairly been criticized for being too sterile and homogenized. "I wanted it to be more luxurious and comfortable."

To make the space more open, like the loft he had previously lived in, Anderson ripped out the closet, expanding the hallway to the bedroom. Insignificant moldings and the carpeting were removed altogether, allowing the concrete shell to take on a more contemporary look. Unnecessary partition walls were eliminated and replaced with see-through floor-to-ceiling shelves and cabinets that Anderson devised with Park Furniture. The kitchen/dining room wall was replaced with a showy pale maple cabinet/countertop with a pass-through opening. A vestibule that doubles as a guest room was separated from the living space by vitrines and bookcases, also prototypes for lines of furniture now produced by Park. This strategy freed perimeter walls that are not broken by windows to showcase Anderson's collection of photography, which he began with the purchase of Joel-Peter Witkin's 1988 *Three Graces*, and other artwork, such as a collection of French wooden airplane models from the 1930s that he discovered in Morocco. Although most of the furniture is freestanding, it looks built-in, giving the condo an uncluttered refinement. "The spareness is designed to highlight each displayed object," explains Anderson. "I don't like to be overloaded. Anything more in this space would make me feel trapped."

FACING PAGE The bedroom is enlivened by broad painted bands of white and dull gold on the walls. The low, Japanese-style bed draws the eye toward the view. RIGHT, TOP The headboard in the bedroom is Anderson's design. RIGHT Display vitrines and bookcases were developed in collaboration with Daven Joy, of Park Furniture. Bookcases in the bedroom, visible from the vestibule, are Park Furniture prototypes. The floor-to-ceiling bookshelves lend a homey warmth to the spare room.

## STEELY/LIU RESIDENCE
### A HOUSE NEAR BUENA VISTA

To understand the design rationale of architect Craig Steely's San Francisco house, it is revealing to know what he did while he was attending school in Italy. "I was studying in Florence, and in my spare time I designed window displays," he says, "including props and sets for the fashion stores on Via Roma." Back in the United States, Steely continued doing displays for Neiman Marcus and Gump's while his wife, Cathy Liu, whom he had met in Italy, became an editor at *Mother Jones* magazine.

At Gump's SOMA workshop, "I found myself actually building the displays I designed," says Steely. Good houses, Steely began to think, were not unlike good window displays, suitably framing the objects within them. So when he found a small, badly planned, but affordable house for the two of them, he knew what to do.

His 1910 no-frills Edwardian had been moved to its present site, a lot barely big enough to hold it; a minuscule space behind the house is just big enough for a cat to stretch in. "This house is an orphan. We have no idea where it came from," he laughs. It had been treated poorly, suffering insensitive remodeling along the way. Pulling it all out and leaving the nine hundred square feet as one giant room wasn't an option. "We didn't want to turn it into a warehouse . . . or an Edwardian reproduction either. It was too late for that," Steely says.

The couple began by erasing obvious mistakes. They stripped painted floors to reveal the original fir and replaced metal windows with wooden ones. In the living room, where the aluminum windows fitted into enlarged bays actually brought in more light, they left them alone. For even more light, they added skylights. For the windows that looked onto a dreary air shaft, they found a type of bottle glass called tulip glass. "It just holds the light beautifully," Steely says. A creamy white paint reflects this bounty of light throughout.

To open sight lines for unobstructed views from end to end, Steely punctured walls rather than removing them and installed glass cases within the openings. Treated this way, the see-through walls have become instant furniture, melting away to create roomy, airy spaces.

ABOVE The coffee table with an open-to-view drawer for displaying found objects. LEFT The glass display cases set within the dining room walls. FACING PAGE A distressed dining table, and the upright chairs that suggest work by Donald Judd are all Steely creations.

"We took the walls out gradually, going from a doorway to a completely open wall. We added back stub walls like Roman pilasters that catch space and light," Steely says.

To create an even greater illusion of space, the architect aimed for heroic, slender proportions for doorways, replacing standard doors with narrower, taller versions fitted with the house's original brass hardware.

The dark hallway that connected the front and back sections of the small house is now a skylit "spine," and the transparent rooms are a play of light and shade. "It seems bigger because you get glimpses of other rooms, but you don't see all the walls. It's a trick I learned from Italian farmhouses," he confesses.

Since he works at home, the front section of the building is an office, the dining table part desk and part dining surface by day. Even the kitchen, which

is adjacent to their bedroom, is planned rationally in the Miesian way, intended to have everything put away when not in use. "It's all public space. We needed to use one hundred percent of it all the time," he says.

The laundry porch off the kitchen, the kind of ragtag room that has been added to virtually every house in San Francisco neighborhoods, got a unique facelift.

"I grew up in the Sierra foothills near Jackson, so I wanted to make this room like a cabin in the city," Steely explains. He widened the doorway to get a better view through the glass backdoor of a magnificent tree in a neighbor's garden just a few feet away, then clad the ceiling with galvanized corrugated sheeting, held in place with fir joists for effect. "It feels more like a porch than it ever did," Steely says.

Without adding square footage, Steely and Liu have visually doubled the size of their home. The way Steely looks at it, even though they couldn't conjure up more land around their little house, and the kitchen is small, "every restaurant and park in the city is our space."

FACING PAGE A skylit passageway leads to the kitchen in the back. Stacked aluminum vessels from India—a sculptural totem—contain grains. The back porch is finished with birch, with galvanized sheeting and fir timbers on the ceiling. Old, paned windows contrast pleasingly with new, tall doors chosen for their heroic proportions. LEFT In the bedroom, a tall wardrobe of remilled redwood and birch is Steely's design. RIGHT, TOP In the living room, a "snowshoe" bookcase is by Steely. RIGHT Salvaged glass doors installed on tracks make compact cabinets.

## ZOLEZZI RESIDENCE
### A HOUSE IN SAUSALITO

The day Craig Zolezzi, a restaurateur with Bay Area connections, decided to return home from Colorado to be closer to his Italian family, he heard of a house for sale not far from Mt. Tamalpais. "I still wanted to be in the country, among the mountains," says the young man. Right away, he bought the old two-story building, which had an uncertain pedigree but a spectacular view. The house, probably from the 1920s—essentially two jogged balloon-frame boxes stacked on a narrow, steep hillside lot—is in Sausalito, a one-time fishing village just across the Golden Gate Bridge from San Francisco.

LEFT A column clad in aluminum is a prominent metal counterpoint to fixed wood and plaster partitions within the interior. Wood-chip composite boards, cut in squares for floor tiles, are laid in random patterns to conceal orthogonal joints and simulate a leaf-strewn forest floor. "Alan's metal furniture developed later, but we always planned to have the furniture laid diagonally in the living room to take advantage of the view," says Fecskes. Concrete steps with high risers that lead to the deck were designed to serve as informal seating. A wooden Madonna in the living room is a baroque nod to his Italian heritage, but the overall spare Japanese aesthetic suits Zolezzi better. Seen through the glazed wall just beyond the wood-burning stove is a narrow reflecting pool recessed within the deck. TOP RIGHT The inscrutable exterior, above, suggests that Zolezzi wanted this loftlike space to be a hideout. BOTTOM RIGHT The furniture, a principal feature of the interior, is designed by Alan Sklansky to serve as sculpture as well as to be utilitarian. An elegant metal-mesh and plywood shelving system incorporates a foldaway desk.

As early as 1869, cottage lots were platted on the steep slopes above Sausalito. The undertaking was soon abandoned when it failed to attract many new residents, even with improved ferryboat connections to the city. It was not until the 1880s that a significant number of houses were erected on the hillside. With Sausalito's increasing appeal, other sites in Marin County, such as Mill Valley and the islandlike setting of Belvedere, were developed along Sausalito's rustic lines, serving city residents through the long months of clement weather as both suburbs and resorts. The informal buildings built in these areas nurtured the taste for rusticity and the relaxed living patterns that have been identified with the Bay Area ever since. Many of the early houses by architects Ernest Coxhead and Willis Polk, perpetrators of the regional rustic modernism fully emerging in the 1940s, were built in Marin County.

Just as San Francisco's proximity to the rugged landscape of Marin and the East Bay drew these architects toward rusticity, it also encouraged them to add urbane refinements in the resort suburbs. Sausalito continues in that spirit today as a satellite township, an urbane suburban enclave. Its hastily built fisherman's cottages, weekend villas, and even a few mansions that hug the steep hills looking out at the bay have become coveted addresses. The relatively sharp changes in grade of the small lots allow both privacy and breathtaking views.

"I love old buildings, but I realized this one had to be rebuilt. I wanted to design every detail . . . even the faucets," Zolezzi says. With San Rafael–based architect Julianna Fecskes, who once worked in Frank Gehry's design office, Zolezzi brainstormed for ways to expand the views yet save the original floor plan; they eventually decided to gut the thousand-square-foot interior and start over.

From the street, only the upper-story box is visible; steps cut into the hillside lead down to the lower floor. "I wanted the front to be like a fort," says Zolezzi, who seeks isolation when he is not working with his family or as a part-time counselor for abused children. "It's a place to be alone in. I spend half the week (at a shelter)

FACING PAGE, LEFT Behind the bed, a walk-through closet leads to the bathroom. FACING PAGE, TOP In the bathroom, more custom features built by Sklansky; a steel sink and metal-mesh cabinets are industrial features. RIGHT A raised bed platform topped with a futon abuts a soaking tub tiled with blue Italian-glass mosaic. Beyond it is an open shower that has views of the Bay Bridge.

with seven other people and a dog!" he says. Clad in rough-sawn cedar interrupted only by a metal front door, Zolezzi's home does seem introverted and forbidding, a foil to the open loftlike plan and sweeping views within.

The keys to the transformation were in enlarging the view-facing windows and installing an open shower, a sunken tub, and a bed platform in the center of the space. In a clockwise spiral, the architect and Zolezzi laid out three interlocked L-shaped spaces: kitchen, dining, and living areas; a large storage and closet area partitioned from view; and an enclosed bathroom connected to the open-to-view shower/tub. The raised bed platform is at the center of the spiral. Plywood baseboards with the grain running horizontally act as subtle directional markers. The narrow double-galley kitchen and a utility room are also enclosed by partitions. Beyond the glazed wall is a deck with outdoor seating; a railing of sheet glass (for unhampered views) is bordered by a narrow reflecting pool that can be lit subtly at night.

Alan Sklansky, an East Bay furniture designer with an architectural background, further shaped the house's contemporary, Japanese-influenced aesthetic under Zolezzi's supervision. Against the south wall, a storage system with a foldaway desk Sklansky designed incorporates metal-mesh screens. A steel and frosted-acrylic screen—suspended from overhead tracks that can be rolled across the room to shield the raised futon bed and open shower from view—more closely resembles shoji screens. An elliptical table and bar stools, all of steel, face a windowless wall where Sklansky's

elegant steel-framed mirror reflects the bay view like ponds in traditional Japanese gardens. The use of Plexiglas, mesh, wood, and other natural materials saves the interior from looking too metal-heavy. "I had the tatami mats," says Zolezzi, pointing to their use as padding for Sklansky's comfortable, adjustable steel-and-wood chaises in the living room.

Surprisingly, for all his reclusiveness, Zolezzi likes to entertain guests. His father, a professional chef who owned the Flytrap restaurant in San Francisco, cooks in the tiny but efficient kitchen for large family gatherings. "Fifty of us gather for Christmas. I have so many nieces and nephews, it's always a great party," says Zolezzi.

FACING PAGE Tatami mats inspired low window seats; an adjustable chaise-style sofa dominates the living space; next to a counter-height elliptical dining table with bar stools, the exterior view reflects in a steel-framed mirror. BELOW The south view.

## SCHINDLER RESIDENCE
### A HOUSE ON POTRERO HILL

When Susan Schindler, who owns the zany South of Market Brain Wash Cafe & Laundromat, first saw the Potrero Hill house she now owns, she felt it wasn't for her. But when she stepped into the pristine, modernist house, which Francis Joseph McCarthy, an exponent of the Bay Region tradition, had designed for Standard Oil executive Chandler Kellogg and his wife in the 1950s, she was seduced. "I knew this house was special right from the start. It took my breath away. I had always wanted to live in an auto-body shop. That's my personality," she laughs. "Instead, I landed in a Hollywood Hills house in San Francisco."

The split-level house was built on a steep corner lot; its site-sensitive L-shaped plan was designed to take in the 180-degree view looking north over the city and east over the bay, and at the same time to shield a two-level courtyard garden set within the L. The longer part of the L contains the living room, a bedroom, and a dressing room and bath. A guest room below this wing leads to another garden at the back of the house. An entry hallway, a small kitchen, a guest bath, and the dining area make up the short arm of the L.

The outdoor spaces, front and back, make this two-bedroom, shed-roof house seem larger than its sixteen hundred square feet of floor space. Walls of glass open the dining/kitchen areas to the enclosed courtyard, and when outside, as Schindler says, "you can still see the city through all the glass." A unique set of giant, painted-wood louvers installed vertically on the western glass wall can be cranked open for the view or closed to shield the living room from street noise or the sun's glare.

"My house has its own personality," says Schindler. Weeks of arranging and rearranging her collection of flea-market finds—a lamp in the shape of the brain, a teapot shaped like a laundry machine, her prized collection of Grateful Dead pictures by Herb Greene, a custom-built rowing machine, and most everything

FACING PAGE Looking east, Schindler can see the city and the bay from her living room. A "wave" chair holds court among fine company: a Gae Aulenti coffee table, and wool-covered chairs designed in the style of Eero Saarinen, made for the old San Francisco Museum of Modern Art. Blown-glass vases from de Vera and a red-and-black Carlos Scarpa vase lend color. A new slab of black granite completes the hearth. ABOVE Outside, the louvers offer instant privacy. RIGHT An Arne Jacobsen egg chair.

that worked wonderfully at her previous loft space—made her realize that they just wouldn't fit in here.

"I realized I had to do some things differently. Buildings can control you," she says, a little put out at having to abandon her free-spirited 1960s aesthetic. With the help of designer Federico de Vera, Schindler began to outfit the house in the austere modernist style to which it once was accustomed.

But de Vera's clean-lined, well-ordered design is not just another 1950s reprise. "I wanted to throw the lines of the architecture into focus," he says, "but I didn't try to slavishly aim for a fifties 'look.' Instead, we mixed things for a period feeling, but at the same time it is completely modern."

FACING PAGE De Vera designed a mantel of solid maple that floats above the fireplace, supported only by a thin steel rod to its left. It takes its cues from the original cantilevered steel hearth, which had to be stripped to bare metal. Above the mantel, he designed a light, removable box of maple with adjustable steel shelves that hold Schindler's collection of detergent cartons from the 1940s, 1950s, and 1960s. ABOVE In the bedroom, a striking, simply conceived maple bed and maple-and-glass side tables are by San Francisco designer Daven Joy. Atop the bedside table is a "brain" lamp with a bare lightbulb. RIGHT A discreet crank turns the louvers.

boxes from the forties, fifties, and sixties, displayed in what is de Vera's most modernist addition to the room. "Susan wanted to make sure she would still have some of her fun things to look at," says de Vera, so carpenter Paul Smith fabricated a flat mantel of solid maple with a shallow recess, to mirror the hearth of black steel, directly below. On it rests a removable, fully adjustable shelving "box" with thick-gauge steel shelves. "I wanted to put all the boxes into one giant box . . . a shape," says de Vera.

Schindler and de Vera agonized over every move, careful not to disturb the precisely detailed house. The original shelving system in the living room was left intact, but the long wooden bookshelves were replaced with narrower brushed steel-and-glass shelves that can be moved to adjust displays of objects. "The original plywood walls had been painted over with this vanilla color before I got here," says Schindler, "but I like it. What gives me a real kick is we've spent all this time and all this money, and it all looks like it was always there."

LEFT The upper garden wraps around an opening designed to bring light to the lower-level guest room. At dusk, the L-shaped wraparound house disappears, its glass walls open to view. BELOW In the dining area, a pencil and watercolor work by Sid Garrison complements a table by Heywood-Wakefield and leather-covered Thonet chairs. FACING PAGE The wood-paneled room downstairs has a copper-clad fireplace . Photograph of Janis Joplin by Herb Greene.

Nearly everything in the house was first moved out. Then, on that blank, streamlined canvas, de Vera painted in the sensuous shapes and colors that make the design.

Some of the old furniture was perfect for the living room. A well-worn 1957 egg chair by Arne Jacobsen, a gift to Schindler from artist Nayland Blake, was revived with new upholstery. Upholsterer Mike Boloyan also rescued a sensuous "wave" chair, another gift, from exile in the garage. To these pieces, de Vera added a collection of original blown glass of his own design, a coffee table by Arte Fontana, and two Eero Saarinen–like chairs designed for the old San Francisco Museum of Modern Art. In the dining area, a couple of Schindler's old, refinished Joe Atkinson chairs were combined with other Thonet armchairs and a Heywood-Wakefield table.

In the bedroom, McCarthy designed a wall of shoji screen–like storage cupboards that break up the surface with an orderly grid. The room itself is narrow and required special care. Here, de Vera asked designer Daven Joy to make a suite of custom furniture. The bed design Schindler chose is one Joy adapted especially for the space. Broad-grained maple-faced boards cut in a simple geometry of rectangles make a handsome bed with a high headboard that allows Schindler to sit back and take in the wall-to-wall view. Opposite the bed is Schindler's collection of detergent

# LOFT LIVING

# HEINSER/CORSON RESIDENCE
## A LIVE/WORK BUILDING IN THE SOMA DISTRICT

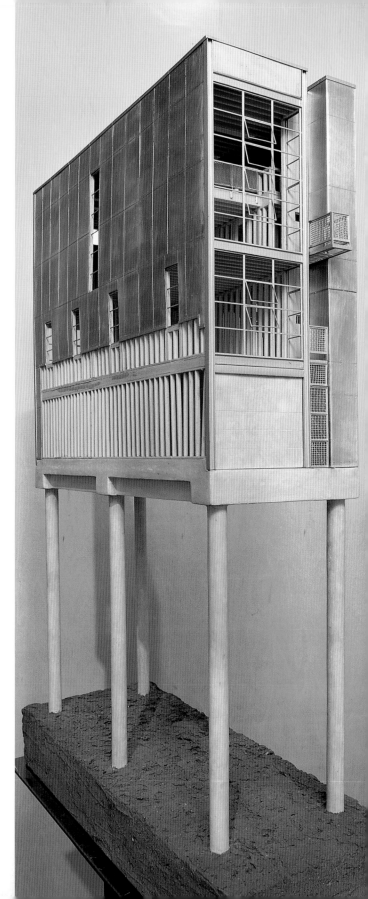

alone build a home in an area that Corson describes as an "urban outback." They had already looked at several remodeled buildings, but, says Corson, "we realized we'd never find our dream loft ready-made in a dream neighborhood."

FACING PAGE Thomas Heinser and Madeleine Corson designed their three-story loft as a place to live and work: a chute for a load-carrying dumbwaiter is covered with low-maintenance galvanized sheet metal. A structural steel frame, left exposed, outlines the building with modernist clarity.
LEFT AND BELOW Skylights and large windows provide natural light for photography; light filters down the open stairwell to lower levels. RIGHT A model on "stilts" shows the building's underground pylons—designed to reach bedrock.

In San Francisco, even a barely usable sliver of downtown land can spark a great deal of interest. When photographer Thomas Heinser spotted someone surveying a narrow, disused parking lot just two doors away from his South of Market photo studio, he moved fast.

"I want to buy it," he told the owner, who was getting ready to unload his back-alley parcel of seemingly useless land. The land changed hands, and before long an austere, slender modernist structure of sheet metal, wood, and glass had sprung up, sandwiched between low-slung 1930s warehouses.

Neither Heinser nor his wife, graphic designer Madeleine Corson, had ever thought they would leave their cozy North Beach neighborhood, let

When they found that an architect had already considered the same live/work site for himself and had drawn up plans for a building close to what they wanted, the situation seemed almost karmic.

"We were very clear about what we needed," says Corson. "We wanted a simple, completely functional loft space with as many windows as possible. We needed a place to live and work, where we could see each other more often. We didn't need too many closed rooms."

Their architect, Richard Stacy, of the local firm Tanner Leddy Maytum Stacy, gave them just that. "Richard changed things himself down the road. It was his baby. He got very involved," says Heinser. "He was the one who decided that it should be an asymmetrical building, with utilities on one side and the open light-filled loft areas on the other side. It was a wonderful step."

Stacy modified the original plan to accommodate most of Heinser and Corson's ideas, including low-maintenance exterior materials and a dumbwaiter to haul Heinser's photographic equipment to and from his studio. The inner workings of the nineteen-foot-wide, forty-two-foot-high building, whose three narrow stories encompass four thousand square feet, are plainly evident through the large industrial windows that form the facade, which has been reinforced with a stabilizing frame made of steel. The garage, the living spaces, and, at the top,

FACING PAGE The structure's middle level is Heinser and Corson's private domain. RIGHT A streamlined galley kitchen separates the living spaces from a bedroom wing in the back. Doorways to the kitchen can be closed off with Plexiglas-and-wood screens hung on tracks.

Heinser's two-level photo studio with a sixteen-foot ceiling are stacked; a shaft of galvanized sheet metal beside the windows and the fire escape houses the dumbwaiter.

Corson's garden studio is in the back. Although it is small, with the touch of a button the glass-paneled garage door that separates the studio from the garden rolls away, expanding the cramped space visually. "It can get drafty, but I like it psychologically that the wall can go away," says Corson. Plywood floors, exposed studs and joists, and a series of

LEFT A door on wheels, which doubles as shelves, pockets behind the wall and rolls easily on overhead tracks.
ABOVE On the third level, Heinser's photo studio, during a rare lull. FACING PAGE, LEFT A new addition includes an office with an unusual bamboo ply floor. RIGHT Between shoots, Heinser provides a place to take a break.

cement and perforated-steel staircases with see-through metal-grating landings complement the building's industrial aesthetic. From his perch high above the South of Market area, Heinser can look down to Corson's studio entrance and discuss lunch plans with her without having to phone.

"Everything in the building is a conscious decision," says Heinser, flaunting his penchant for order and precision. "Both Richard and I loved working on the details."

Corson, after initial wariness, has learned to love the transitory nature of her new world. "I'm from the Midwest, and in some weird way, this area is like that. After hours, the wide streets are empty; it seems almost rural."

# HUTTON RESIDENCE
## A LOFT IN THE MISSION DISTRICT

When interior designer Gary Hutton first saw the Mission District warehouse where he now lives, it echoed the sketchy neighborhood—it was broken up into a series of dark, jerry-built rooms made of plywood and masking tape. Perhaps that's why he was able to lease it so cheaply. "It's no bargain now … but the neighborhood has changed too," Hutton says.

In the last few years, new businesses like the Slow Club and the Universal Cafe began to alter the area. Now, on a warm evening, Hutton frequently finds an open garage bedecked with lounge chairs, a boom box blaring rap music, and the owners standing at a barbecue, turning hot dogs, while outside the Universal Cafe a chic clientele emerges from fancy Porsches. "It's beautiful … it doesn't happen too often elsewhere in the city," Hutton says. The change in the neighborhood has been fortuitous, since Hutton works out of his home and spends a lot of time there.

Originally a commercial space, the building came with two restrooms. One was transformed into a chic bathroom, and the plumbing for the other was converted so the room could function as a kitchen. The concrete walls were painted a neutral off-white, and the

FACING PAGE A slipcased banquette and a checkered carpet define the living space in one corner of Gary Hutton's loft space. A tall, bronzed lamp stand and a vaguely African conical side table are Hutton's own designs. THIS PAGE In the entryway, Hutton paired a cowhide and wood book cabinet with a framed mirror he designed, which leans against the wall near a white John Dickenson table.

In one corner, a platform bed veneered to resemble a Beidermeier piece suggests a bedroom; and in another, a large L-shaped slipcased banquette defines the living space. "Slipcovers never fit really well, so they make furniture more casual. The banquette is in great shape, so now I have an option," Hutton says.

Perhaps because he studied art with sculptors Robert Arneson and Manuel Neri, Hutton thinks sculpturally. "I like form and texture," he says. Objects are arranged in studied, deliberate compositions. But, Hutton insists, "My collection of things has a lot to do with remembrances. It is a chronicle of my life." There's always room in Hutton's space for gifts from friends, travel mementos, and the many books he finds at thrift stores during walking tours. A cowhide and wood cabinet in front of a large mirror he designed for a show house contains his design books. A John Dickenson table came from a friend's estate. "I encourage my clients to surround themselves as I do, with objects that are important in that way," he says.

cement floors, originally covered with carpet and ugly vinyl tile, were sandblasted and custom stained. "I just wax them regularly for a nice sheen," says Hutton.

To cordon off a section of the thousand-square-foot space for his desk and home office, Hutton designed a see-through wall of horizontal sections with gaps between them.

This "screen" is the only space divider. Hutton's collection of personal memorabilia, and furniture he has designed for himself or for show houses, are arranged into informal, convivial islands within the more-or-less open space.

Living and working in the same space can have its obvious distractions, and anyone who does live and work in the same space has to go "home." Hutton draws an invisible line. "I have to separate the two consciously. It's a necessary ritual," he says. "I turn out the lights at my desk so it's dark in that area. I adjust the blinds, change some arrangements, and decompress." In effect, he commutes home. "And I even use a different phone at night," Hutton laughs.

FACING PAGE A platform bed, veneered to simulate a Beidermeier look, serves as additional seating during the day. A see-through wall of horizontal sections spaced evenly apart shields Hutton's home office from view. The kitchen is visible in the back. A built-in bookshelf/bar screens off the bathroom door. ABOVE Hutton displays textural groupings of beautifully crafted finds from thrift stores; a mirrored coffee table is from the 1930s. RIGHT On the wall, beside a dining table he designed, are paintings he found at auction. Brno armchairs around the table are by Mies van der Rohe.

## BRAYTON/BURNHAM RESIDENCE
### A HOUSE IN THE FILLMORE DISTRICT

Even before you enter, an arresting black-and-white collage of fabric patterns covering the wide garage door of this new San Francisco home announces there's an artist within.

"This is the only house I've ever designed," says Richard Brayton, an interior designer who, with his artist-wife, Mardi Burnham, owns the narrow three-story structure hidden away in a side alley in the Upper Fillmore.

LEFT Richard Brayton and his wife, artist Mardi Burnham's adventurous three-story "loft": A colonnade of burnt-orange walls defines the hallway library that leads to Burnham's art studio. BELOW A circular skylight brings in light. RIGHT The living space and Burnham's atelier occupy the middle floor.

"Mardi does the color in our office," says Brayton, whose firm, Brayton and Hughes, has won several national design awards. Brayton thought the garage door would be a great place for her painting, but the project evolved into an installation that took over three months to complete, a smaller cousin of the eighty-foot mural she did for Chiron, a biotech company in Emeryville.

"I got to know the neighbors while doing this mural," says Burnham cheerfully. Composed of enlarged copies of fabric patterns collected at the office, the collage is waterproofed with Rhoplex glue. The combination of caning patterns, tiles, lace, and even Fortuny fabrics looks like artful graffiti over metal.

Two years ago, when the couple thought they would build a home, they knew exactly what they didn't want. They had previously lived in a once-condemned Victorian that they gutted to feel like an open-plan loft space, a remodel that proved to be far from ideal. "With children, we learned that a wide open space doesn't work at all," says Burnham. "There's noise everywhere." This time, they wanted rooms where she could paint and where they could both be inspired.

"We lived in a house painted all white for eight years," Burnham adds. All that time, they intended to paint the walls in different colors but could never agree on a shade. "This time I said, 'let's do the color right away.' Of course, I wanted a cornflower blue floor, but Rich wouldn't have it." They settled on the colors of fall leaves they saw on a trip to Mammoth Lake, and these are echoed on burnt-orange columns and walls of cornflower blue and rust. The bright color is perfectly balanced by the high-ceilinged spaces within the three-story house, imbuing the bright, skylit interior with a year-round festive air.

In a sense, even though Burnham has an atelier tucked away on the second floor of their new house, the entire building has become a laboratory for her work. The colored walls act as a backdrop for the couple's eclectic collection of things gathered during their travels: A birdcage from Hong Kong, a naive painting from Hawaii, and an old trunk that's been around the world with them are displayed along with Burnham's own artwork—abstract collages gilded like fake money used in Chinese rituals. "Collections don't have to be valuable, but they have to be personal," says Brayton.

Educated in architecture, Brayton also saw his new house as a ground for experiment and as a chance to build his favorite kind of structure, a modern house.

FACING PAGE Facing the alleyway, the atelier windows, directly above Burnham's garage-door mural, lend the facade an industrial air; a peaked skylight crowns the main stairwell, bringing light to every level. RIGHT In the living room, a model of the building rests on built-in bookshelves. BELOW The fireplace chimney is shared by the garden fireplace below.

"All of a sudden you are your own best client," he says. "It's still hard to talk clients into modernism."

Brayton's house became a simple block of living spaces wrapped by an L-shaped stairwell, with interior spaces divided cleverly to bring in light to the lowest floor and to give the space an illusion of greater height and volume.

Its facade is an asymmetrical grid of warehouse windows (standard aluminum extrusions, double-glazed for noise and heat) and a tall entryway that mimics the adjacent turn-of-the-century Victorians that were originally built as squatter's shacks, without indoor plumbing but with tall, elegant entryways unusual in small houses. "There's a studio Corbusier designed that's part of the inspiration for this facade," says Brayton. The streetside grid is a clue both to the different levels within the house and to their spatial organization. The garage, a kitchen, a powder room, and a family room are on the ground level; Burnham's atelier, a library corridor, and the living room are above them; and finally, at the top, symmetrically arranged bedrooms sit on each side of the central, skylit landing. Below the skylight, a circular cutout in the landing floor (temporarily encircled by a protective railing) is intended for a spiral staircase that will lead from the level below up to a planned roof garden. The open living spaces are wrapped by walls or by floor-to-ceiling shelving built in opposing L shapes around them. "It was a game of balance and proportion," explains Brayton.

Narrow side windows modulate the west face of the building. In the back, Brayton was able to squeeze in an exterior fireplace for a tiny back garden.

The most dramatic aspect of the design, however, besides its use of color, is a metal staircase that rises from the street entrance connecting every level of the house, with landings that overlook family spaces directly below the living room. "This was the street transposed into the house," says Brayton. Essentially, it's a European-style covered alley crowned with its own skylight. "It's narrow and has its own circulation. Naturally, it made sense to have a stairway that let in light," says Brayton. The light from overhead heightens the sense of open volumes, and diamond-shaped trusses, added for seismic support, cast dramatic shadows. "There was nothing difficult about the skylight, which was custom-made at a sixty-degree pitch," says Brayton. "Even the painted steel stairs you can get from a catalog."

The overall impression is one of spontaneity—much like that of the neighborhood, with upscale stores cheek by jowl with rib joints and jazz bars. "Here we feel like we live in the city, and we can really get immersed in it," says Brayton. "And I'm glad now that the floors aren't blue," laughs Burnham.

FACING PAGE A circular cutout in the top landing leaks light from a skylight overhead into a study. In the bedroom, a bed from Limn and travel mementos. ABOVE A compact bathroom with a black canvas curtain is centered between the bedrooms.

## THE CLOCK TOWER LOFTS
### LIVE/WORK LOFTS IN THE SOMA DISTRICT

The open-plan interiors espoused by high modernists like Le Corbusier have become ubiquitous in artists' work studios with living arrangements. In San Francisco's South of Market Area, artists had been converting raw industrial loft spaces into live/work spaces for over two decades before the conversion of this 1907 warehouse, with its landmark clock tower, near the approach to the Bay Bridge. The big difference in this conversion was that a developer, Rick Holliday, transformed the grassroots model into a marketable concept for the 1990s, turning large, unused blocks of industrial space into multi-unit lofts at one go.

The Clock Tower—actually three interconnected buildings—once housed the Schmidt Lithograph Company, whose designers produced classic California fruit-crate labels. The original three-story brick and timber plant was expanded to include a six-story concrete structure. Finally, to signal the company's ongoing success, the 170-foot-high steel-frame clock tower was added. The 1990 conversion transformed the structures—230,000 square feet in all—into 127 open floor-plan spaces that offered tenants live/work units with views of the freeway and the bay.

Architect David Baker, hired to design the conversion, set the modern, somewhat unbridled aesthetic tone. Baker says he emulated "the spatial experience of New York City's Soho lofts," where the basic model of open space with a suspended loft bedroom allowed myriad lifestyle interpretations.

Space in the three buildings was divided into forty-four distinct floor plans, repeated as infrequently as possible. Baker likens this group of buildings to an old city quarter, or arrondissement, with its spatial variations. A labyrinth of passageways connects the different spaces. "Modern cities are too rational," Baker says. "It's nice to lose your way once in a while."

The brick walls of the oldest structure are left exposed, as are the concrete columns of the six-story addition that followed it. Directly below the still-functioning tower clock, a dilapidated Bavarian-style beer hall, once reserved for the Schmidts and their friends, was converted into the kind of penthouse one would

FACING PAGE Clear glass in the clock face allows a view of ships passing in the bay.
RIGHT The namesake clock tower looms above the penthouse, just below the clock room itself.

expect in a steel-frame high-rise, with magnificent views of the bay and the freeway swirling below.

Artists hired by Baker, drawing on Bay Area craft and regional modern traditions, have made this space more than a "machine for living"; they have created a warmer and more eclectic environment than most new projects of this scale would support. An inner courtyard is landscaped with a row of stately palm trees; usable art, such as mailboxes made by Paco Prieto, flanks a gently sloping ramp in the entry lobby; a sculptural freestanding metal staircase by Jeff and Larissa Sand leads from the lobby up to lofts above street level; hand-worked sink tops by Buddy Rhodes are installed in every bathroom.

In one model unit, designer Carol Hacker worked with the light and industrial spareness of concrete walls and floors, choosing a mix of contemporary and traditional furniture to achieve a modern aesthetic. A diaphanous silk-screened curtain shields the bedroom loft from strong light pouring in from the floor-to-ceiling warehouse windows. Most of the spaces, however, were allowed to remain relatively pristine, to be converted fully by individual users over time.

FACING PAGE In a model unit, Carol Hacker displays crafts and furniture: Randy Castellon/Zinc Details' wood pedestal; leather and bentwood chair by Arcimboldo designed by architect Bernardo Urquieta; knock-down dining table by Anne Fougeron; mural by Art Decor. COUNTERCLOCKWISE FROM RIGHT In the bathroom, a sink top by Buddy Rhodes; at the Second Street entrance, a poured-concrete ramp allows wheelchair access. Mailboxes by artist Paco Prieto border the path; Jeff and Larissa Sand's futuristic staircase of aluminum and steel; silk-screened drapes by Steven Gordon Fabrics shield the bedroom loft, with a bed by Eric Powell.

## CHAZEN RESIDENCE
### AN ADDITION ON RUSSIAN HILL

Anyone who has ever tried to build or modify a structure in this historic Russian Hill block of houses, which includes structures by Wurster and Polk and other early Bay Region style residences, could have told Larry Chazen to anticipate a battle when he planned an addition to his home.

Chazen, a financial advisor, proposed building a detached dwelling directly behind his own; however, although zoning laws permitted it, neighbors protested the loss of bay views that would result. The original design was too large, too towering, and too invasive, they said. Architect Joseph Esherick, who lives a few blocks from the site, described it as "ill conceived." The Walters house, a 1951 Wurster, Bernardi & Emmons townhouse informally organized to take maximum advantage of the views, stands to the east of Chazen's north-sloping site and would surely have lost its grandstand view of the Golden Gate Bridge from the kitchen and a study.

Chazen's architect, George Hauser, devised a compromise: He located the addition deep within the lot, displacing the owner's well-established Japanese garden. "Naturally, the neighbors were willing to give up their views of the garden if they could keep the bay views intact," says Hauser.

The new structure is deliberately built low on the sloping site, its floor space literally carved out of the hill. The inverted three-story design turns this complicated maneuver into a distinct advantage. "This house is like the Wurster house in a way—it is also a series of stacked, merging boxes," says Hauser. The garage, just west of the entry passage on the south side, a living room, and a dining room with an open galley kitchen are contained in a box with windows on three sides that is entirely above the surface. It rests above partially subterranean boxes that form the two bedroom levels below, reversing the idea of loft bedrooms. "For an opening, you usually cut a window in the box. But the lower boxes are displaced here, and enclosed. We had to pour twenty-foot-high retaining walls to hold back the hill," explains Hauser.

To let in light, the architect imploded the core of the house into a three-story atrium light well. Using all the glass he was allowed at the uppermost level, where the best views are, he capped the well with a skylit roof that pours light into the family room three flights below. Floor-to-ceiling windows open the west and north walls to views. Doors open onto a wide north deck that has oversized flower boxes to make up for the lost garden. A showy maple and

FACING PAGE A Russian Hill addition cants, soars, and opens its walls to views. Custom details—exposed metal joints and braces, steel mantels and hearths, and an open galley kitchen of maple plywood—push the space's modernist, industrial aesthetic in a neighborhood of historic Bay Region homes. RIGHT Unpainted Eterboard exterior siding, metal windows, and an open wood-and-metal staircase leading to bedrooms below, give the house a loftlike air. ABOVE RIGHT Chazen's original home has also been given a facelift to look more like the addition.

custom-steel staircase wraps around the skylit central well to the lower floors. The cantilevered living room floor is suspended over the family room, supported by composition-lumber bends—a modernist trick that mirrors inverted Gothic flying buttresses. The fragmented outer walls seem to be the only fixed elements.

The illusion is one of a building whose structural elements are arranged, rather than built. Despite the clearly expressed joints of its vertical members and the horizontal planes of its barely suggested rooms, the building's suspended floors seem as if they could shift easily to accommodate yet another view.

LEFT Architect George Hauser devised an atrium stairwell to bring light in. ABOVE Interior designer Leslie Bahr complements the unfinished-mineral-fiber Eterboard around the fireplace with a patterned sisal rug; the coffee table is a George Nelson design. FACING PAGE Pale green parallel-strand lumber posts, custom plate connectors, painted metal windows, natural maple floors, and oiled steel mantels and hearths emphasize the raw spontaneity of the design.

BRINGING THE OUTDOORS IN

# BERGGRUEN RESIDENCE

## A HOUSE IN THE WINE COUNTRY

long before they were valued by the art world. He even offered to build her a studio among the vineyards.

Berkeley architects Richard Fernau and Laura Hartman created a closely knit, convivial cluster of friendly buildings—a bunkhouse, a cookhouse, and a lodge—surrounding Berggruen's cottage on a wooded lot sandwiched between two creeks on the edge of a vineyard. The original cottage, completely rebuilt and painted red, claims the center of this complex of structures. The tower studio and outbuildings stand around it, attached or arranged almost haphazardly, as though each was added as the need arose, perhaps mimicking by design what often happens to the simple wood-frame buildings in the valley. The device that sets this building apart—interpreting vernacular forms and even building techniques for modern living spaces—has become the hallmark of

Napa painter Helen Berggruen's house often has unannounced visitors, strangers who are drawn inexorably to its bright colors, storage-shed metal siding, and unusual assemblage of rooftops and gateways.

Alone in the topmost room of her three-story house, with its views of vineyards, she likes to paint the surrounding landscape, juxtaposing those pictures with still-life studies worked in bright, midday-in-the-Caribbean colors that echo the house's palette.

When Berggruen left New York during the 1970s, she also quit Robert Wilson's theater company, with which she had toured Europe. In the West, she joined a new avant-garde group close to her 1920s farmer's cottage on her acre of land in Napa.

In the calm of these surroundings, Berggruen began to paint as a hobby, much encouraged by her father, Heinz Berggruen, famous for selling prints by twentieth-century artists such as Picasso and Matisse

THIS PAGE A large opening forms a dramatic gateway to the inner courtyard. FACING PAGE Metal siding reminiscent of storage sheds, and clapboard walls painted red, blue-green, and yellow give the impression of a cluster of separate buildings.

much of Fernau & Hartman's work. The architects practice what they call "reluctant regionalism," an environmentally responsive architecture rooted in the pragmatism of vernacular California architecture.

In this approach, spaces such as living rooms, bedrooms, and kitchens are often reassembled in unusual independent sequences to reflect changes in the way we live. In a more recent example, a celebrated descendant of the Berggruen house, the architects designed, for a group of retirees, a compound of discrete pavilions linked together for communal living by stairs and bridges.

FACING PAGE In the living room, Berggruen's own fauvist artwork is inspired in part by Indian miniature painting. ABOVE A Bill Baldewicz hutch stands near a wood-burning Rais stove. RIGHT In the kitchen, the wall treatments and the verdigris paint on the custom wood cabinets are muted, but Berggruen's penchant for rich color is satisfied by a collection of Bauer ware. The freestanding kitchen stove centered within the space has a flue that swerves to miss the ridge beam.

travels in India and Afghanistan and an eighteenth-century Indian miniature painting are mingled among flea-market finds.

"When this house was built, I envisioned it as a kind of magnet … an oasis for artist friends," says Berggruen. Now, with fine printer Emily McVarish, who shares the house and works on her own art there, Berggruen has the kind of creative refuge she had hoped for, away from the distractions of San Francisco, where she grew up. Like a character in a novel who develops a will of its own, the house is brokering new friendships for Berggruen. It's become harder to keep uninvited admirers out, but Berggruen doesn't mind too much because, she says, "If they like the house, we usually like them."

While the tower room implies an ascetic bent, the rest of Berggruen's house better reflects her expansive nature, and the design allows as much for living outdoors as in. Doors and windows in the living room open onto a private patio, where friends who sometimes come up from the city gather for parties. One view from the living room is of tall oaks that shelter an elaborate trellised barbecue, and even the quiet, secluded, out-of-sight work spaces have broad, inspiring views of the busy vineyards around the valley.

Some unusual features make the interior a lively experience. A Dutch front door reinforces the inside/outside theme, and white ceilings follow the rise and fall of the roof lines like elaborately folded origami. The walls have special finishes created by artist friends; painted built-in bookshelves and kitchen cabinets, as well as pine walls whitewashed to show off the grain, all show an artist's hand.

The furniture includes a few pieces by artist Bill Baldewicz made especially for Berggruen. Rugs from

FACING PAGE A double Dutch door lets visitors into a vestibule used as a study. It is spare, like a Philip Glass stage set, with a few pieces of art as key players. Architects Fernau & Hartman designed the wall sconces. Stairs lead to small bedrooms, and up another flight is Berggruen's studio. ABOVE Works in progress inside Berggruen's tower studio. RIGHT A space-saving sleeping nook is equipped with overhead bookshelves, and drawers below for storing extra blankets.

# FERNAU/CUNNIFF RESIDENCE
## A HOUSE IN THE BERKELEY HILLS

When Sarah Cunniff, a lawyer for Levi's, and architect Richard Fernau started to look for an affordable house in the North Berkeley hills, they didn't know that they would settle for a humble 1950s two-level cottage that the neighbors considered a tear-down.

It was a very awkward, introverted house that seemed as if it were embarrassed to be on the road. With only a four-foot-deep front garden, it had a cramped urban look in what is still a mostly rural neighborhood with large front and back yards. The house looked worse inside than it did outside. It had cheap-looking mirror-glass tile and an acoustical ceiling probably added in the 1970s.

"The original design was all drawn on two sheets," says Fernau. The small, eight-hundred-square-foot house was probably intended to be affordable when it was built, and it contained a tiny compact kitchen and a built-in Murphy bed. Its two-story, used-brick chimney flanked the clapboard facade; a small window was cut into the shingled wall above the standard garage door. "But it had a folksy quality to it," says Fernau.

In addition to a large living and dining room that mitigated the overall small size of the house, there were other virtues. Just behind the house, the hill sloped down to a running creek, and towering redwoods shielded neighboring homes. This was some-

thing the couple couldn't pass up. The contrast of the sporadic sounds of car traffic right outside their house with the music of the creek that flowed in the woods behind it appealed greatly to the couple.

The biggest aesthetic challenges were to make the front more in keeping with the neighboring cottages and discreet bungalows and to design something dramatically different in the back. "We had to make the house more itself … sort of rewrite the fifties and erase the seventies," says Fernau.

To make the house liveable while they drew up plans for remodeling it, Fernau and Cunniff "used $5,000 and a lot of magic." The magic in this case was

TOP LEFT From the street, Richard Fernau and Sarah Cunniff's North Berkeley home looks like the simple 1950s cottage it used to be. LEFT & ABOVE The enclosed front porch doubles as the children's playroom. FACING PAGE At the back, there's a surprise ending: a dramatic open-air bedroom with a roll-away wall. A redwood post blends in with the surrounding woods.

mostly paint. They painted the tiny kitchen and the shingles in front and reworked a Dutch front door. Soon, even the neighbors began to like the house. "People stopped us to ask about the colors, or they'd say, 'I've changed my walking route so I can see the house,'" says Cunniff.

The old chimney came down during the 1989 earthquake, and that really started the physical transformation of the house. They put in a new fireplace and replaced the chimney with a cased-in flue that echoes the original; in place of the old, rickety front stairway, they added a porched mud room that doubles as a play den for their son Owen. To open the view through the house, a pinched doorway at the back and the front living room windows were both enlarged. The lower panels of the new floor-to-ceiling windows were sandblasted for privacy.

"To see thirty-five feet of space inside gives you the illusion of a bigger house and a different view on either end," says Fernau, who uses this axial design tool in his work. At Fernau & Hartman Architects in Berkeley, where he is a partner, he prefers designs that respond flexibly to a site. "An axial solution is not the whole grammar of architecture," he says, convinced that if a house's plan is entirely revealed, it takes the mystery out. "A good house has to be experienced gradually, you have to taste its parts."

During the remodeling, the couple and their four-year-old son camped in the big living room, where the built-in bed had originally been. On occasion, they would sleep on the small deck overlooking the creek. Sleeping outdoors gave the couple their best idea for the house. When they decided to expand the garage level toward the back of the house to add a

real bedroom for themselves, Fernau designed a roll-away wall that projects outside the building envelope when it is opened. Their small room thus opens onto a cantilevered sleeping porch directly below the upstairs studio. Another room was added below the bedroom itself, creating a third level that has direct access to the creek. Now, nine months out of the year, Fernau and Cunniff sleep outside, suspended among the redwoods. "Conventional master bedrooms are a terrible waste of space," Fernau says. When their bed

FACING PAGE A model of Fernau and Cunniff's house is displayed in the austere living space. ABOVE Tall windows bring light into the big living and dining room. In the background, the old bedroom turned den: Fernau converted its deck into an airy office.

ture. It is improvisation. It is ragged like jazz when you remodel; there is a thrill and an unexpected quality for me that regular architecture doesn't have," says Fernau. His attitude is appropriate, because in the case of this house, improvisation was frequent. The old structure is out of square, and new custom cabinets and a lectern at the head of the new stairwell had to be installed using decorative shims. The biggest challenge, however, was a redwood log that Fernau had acquired from a friend and stored outside for four years. His decision to use it as a support post for the upstairs studio turned out to be a logistical nightmare. The log had to be put in place by hand because cranes could not make it down the steep slope, and the contractors refused to install it. "I could tell there was real fear there of someone being crushed," says Fernau. Always resourceful,

(on wheels) is outside, the rest of the room becomes an open space for yoga and meditation, and an indoor playing field for Owen.

The new porch "is actually the memory of the old deck," says Fernau, a student of philosphy. "One starts to forget the old details." He deliberately included a concrete cavity in the design that will be filled and sealed off as a memory capsule. Rocks found during trips to Japan are also preserved, embedded in the concrete steps that lead down to the creek, where Owen has pitched a play tent.

The additions feel like random, spontaneously built tree houses. "I have a theory of jazz and architec-

he found an expert builder at Tassajara Zen Center in Marin County who had experience with such things. "He essentially built a wooden highway with a block and tackle," says Fernau, who describes the man as an unflappable Zen hippie. "He did it very calmly, wearing sandals."

Fernau and Cunniff are minutes away by car from their Berkeley offices, and a short bicycle ride or a brisk jog away from Tilden Regional Park; yet at home, they are in the heart of the woods. "You can hear the creek most of the year, and then the birds," says Fernau.

FACING PAGE One wall of the couple's bedroom slides open; it cantilevers out within the soaring redwoods, allowing easy access to a sleeping porch. Modernist classics—a chair by Arne Jacobsen and a stool by Alvar Aalto—are paired with a bed on wheels that rolls out onto the porch. ABOVE LEFT A red lectern at the head of the new stairs that lead to the lower additions is shimmed into place. ABOVE The couple's older son, Owen, shares his room with the baby, who sleeps in a custom pull-out crib, a Fernau design. RIGHT The cantilevered bedroom wall.

# NAPIER RESIDENCE

## A HOUSE IN ROSS, MARIN COUNTY

"I think the interior is the most important part of the house," muses San Francisco architect Joseph Esherick. "I am not indifferent to the exterior, but fortunately I have been lucky to have clients who want places to live in."

Esherick's houses, large or small, are light-filled, open spaces that are modernist in their lack of fussy ornament. Stylistically and philosophically, they have much in common with the Bay Area vernacular that was established early this century by architects such as

Bernard Maybeck and Ernest Coxhead and evolved further by William Wurster and Gardner Dailey (in whose office Esherick worked as a young man).

"The principal qualities a house ought to have are flexibility and changeability," says Esherick. "That should be such that it generally stays in the background. People and the things they do are far more important than any building." Taking that concept and specific site conditions as his cues, Esherick resists designs with preconceived notions of order or style. The exteriors of his houses are not always pretty, but the interiors are much admired by the people who use them and have also won him the coveted Gold Medal from the American Institute of Architects.

When Fran and David Napier, a retired couple, decided to rebuild the rambling one-story structure on a heavily wooded ridge in Marin County, which they had built and lived in since the 1970s, they approached the firm Esherick Homsey Dodge and Davis. They had concluded that their present house was not sited conveniently because it straddled an east-west ridge on a two-acre site that was split between two ecotones—the southern side was a dry zone covered in live oaks and madrones; the northern

FACING PAGE Fran and David Napier's Marin County hillside house is designed to mesh with its surroundings more completely over time; trellises will be covered in vines. ABOVE At the entrance facade, red earth–colored stucco cladding and green-stained wood harmonize with the surroundings. RIGHT Working to preserve the landscape and trees in the ecotones on each side of the ridge, Esherick designed two buildings that house public and private sections; an enclosed bridge partially supported by steel piers straddles a landscaped outcropping between the living and bedroom wings of the house, forming a breezeway below. Window frames placed on the outside make the bridge appear larger and more transparent from the inside.

looked their extensive garden. "I loved the views from the old house, but I didn't like seeing the underside of the cantilevered deck as we approached the house," says David. "We also wanted to double the space we'd had before," Fran adds.

Their wish list included display spaces for travel mementos, room for raising his tropical fish, and an arts and crafts room with ample storage for her decorative boxes made from mosses, acorns, and bark found during walks on the wooded property. "I am not able to work out of chaos," says Fran. They wanted a home that would meet these requirements, and not something ostentatious designed expressly to impress people.

With the landscape design firm Christiansen-Arner, Esherick planned the new house, slightly lower on the site and integrated among new plantings set into the diverse environments. The couple's swimming pool and landscaping, flower and vegetable plots, fishponds, rock gardens, and forest paths were left undisturbed. In deference to the site, Esherick canted the house not just for light and views of the bay, but to leave the trees intact. Unlike most of his other houses, he clad this one in fire-resistant earth-colored stucco instead of wood. "We thought of using concrete," says David, "but that would have been too costly."

"We built it as if it were two houses," says Esherick. Working with the site's natural contours using a footprint that is virtually the same as the original

side, a wet redwood forest. The many steps that led from their separate garage to their front door were a hardship they had endured for too long, and the house was cold in the winter and too hot in the summer.

For Esherick, these were dream clients. When the Napiers, one-time entrepreneurs who ran a vast employment agency, came in for the first of over fifty meetings with Esherick (he always draws plans with the clients present) and project architect Glennis Briggs, they were prepared with a dossier of information and space requirements that met Esherick's own design criteria. They wanted to save their ten

solar panels, for example, and they felt deeply vested in the gardens and walkways they had developed over many years. "The importance of landscape . . . you can't talk too much about it," notes Esherick.

Having lived on the site for fifteen years, the couple knew the light and weather conditions well. They knew where the best views were and, passionate cooks, they yearned for a new kitchen that over-

ABOVE In the breakfast area, banquette cushions are covered in leather. A wraparound shelf of black slate is a natural foil for displaying Fran Napier's rotating displays of found objects: bark, ostrich eggs, and bird skeletons. FACING PAGE A black-slate floor unifies the breakfast area and study, both open to the main deck above the front porch. Slate cladding extends to the ceiling at the fireplace wall. Artwork by Sausalito artist Woody Biggs; Eames chair and ottoman; leather-covered Le Corbusier–style sofa.

the floors, and black granite surrounds the fireplace. A blue carpet chosen by Esherick's interior designer, Robin Potampa-Ziv, contrasts against the strict simplicity of the interior while highlighting the Napiers' old favorites—an Eames lounge chair and ottoman and a new Le Corbusier–style couch. A monochromatic palette prevails in the living/dining spaces, which have elegant wood floors.

Esherick, noted for his skill in handling light, modulated varying degrees of natural illumination in different rooms. In the living spaces, windows are employed to bring in light as well as to direct attention toward the view; in the understated bedrooms, views are the principal focus.

For Esherick, the Napier house—open to nature yet strong enough to withstand high winter winds—represents the culmination of fifty years of thinking about architecture as something carved out of the light, the trees, and the wind. "These aren't the usual ingredients of architecture," Esherick has been known to say, "but they are the important ones."

house, Esherick created living and work spaces in the front wing that are connected by an enclosed bridge—that crosses over a rock outcropping—to two stories of bedrooms overlooking the redwoods in the back. The bridge, with its glazed walls and comfortable banquette seating, overlooks a running-brook fountain and becomes an area of repose. It is infinitely more than a passageway. A garage tucked under a broad porch provides easy access to the house from the cars. Inside, the living/dining room is not too large, elegantly scaled with Esherick's preferred eleven-foot ceiling heights. The breakfast/study area, with its built-in banquettes and floor-to-ceiling bookshelves, opens onto a spacious trellised front porch that is accessed through enormous wood and glass doors. In the study, black slate covers

THIS PAGE In the living room, a black-granite fireplace complements sturdy steel-sash windows. Chairs are covered in Donghia fabric. The acrylic-on-canvas painting *In a Boy's Dream* is by Wesley Kimler. The coffee table is made from a fallen madrone from the property. The crisp white, tiled bath frames a view of the woods. FACING PAGE In the dining room, *Yellow Morning*, an acrylic-on-canvas piece reminiscent of Helen Frankenthaler's work, is by Robert Gonzales.

## ROSENTHAL/MURPHY RESIDENCE
### A HOUSE IN NORTH BERKELEY

The design of a building, Stanley Saitowitz tells his students at the University of California, Berkeley, should spring naturally from the geography of its location and the building materials at hand. "I am interested in exposing the essential nature of each particular situation—in turning the site, through building, into a state of mind," says the San Francisco–based architect. "I like having the opportunity to work with gardens. I grew up on a big piece of land in Transvaal, in South Africa, where we grew our own vegetables. It was part of living. When I first came to

FACING PAGE For Rosenthal and Murphy, Saitowitz designed a multilevel house that mimics the existing garden's topography. BELOW Typically, Saitowitz avoids thin laminates, which peel away, choosing materials that are solid. Surprisingly, for this Berkeley house, the architect chose stucco for the exterior, and paint for interior walls. RIGHT More in character is a rich mahogany floor abutting a cast-concrete vestibule with a bench built-in over a cavity for shoes.

LEFT In the living space, an Eileen Gray occasional table, Eames chairs, and a contemporary sofa and chairs. In the raised dining area next to an open kitchen is a Le Corbusier table with Arne Jacobsen side chairs reissued by Knoll, all from The Magazine. ABOVE Partly shut metal "blinders," which echo the pattern of palm fronds, are intended to direct the eye toward bay views. TOP A deck and trellis detail. FACING PAGE Stairs echo level changes outside.

America, I landed in New York. I was fascinated, but California was more gardenlike."

Serendipitously, Larry Rosenthal, a scholar living in Berkeley, and his wife, Ann Murphy, a dance critic, came to Saitowitz when they bought a leftover, fan-shaped garden with mature palm trees just a few blocks from where they lived. It was, they thought, exactly the right setting to build a home to work in as well as to raise their two children.

For Saitowitz, it also represented a perfect garden site, one with context, history, and predetermined alignments. "Most of my work is a continuation of the Bay Area tradition. Maybeck talked about the building as a garden, rather than as architecture," says Saitowitz. However, if he has a linear connection with Maybeck's philosophy, there is none aesthetically: "I am more interested in oriental ideas—the emptiness, the austerity of Japanese architecture."

Clearly a modernist of the Mies, Le Corbusier, and Wright schools, Saitowitz's challenges were to integrate a new building within a neighborhood established with arts and crafts–style bungalows and to minimize its impact on land that the neighborhood had long considered public—a community garden—before the current owners bought it.

Saitowitz describes the design process as a gradual erasure of boundaries. What evolved was a low-lying, multilevel, boomerang-shaped courtyard house that steps up the sloping site, mimicking its gradient. Unlike those of many Mediterranean-style predecessors, this unique garden is not in the center, but runs through the house. Seen from the street, the house seems to straddle the left (north) edge of the site discreetly; the front "arm" floats to the other side,

leaving the old palms intact and the garden accessible and open to view. The topography essentially becomes the form of the house: the floor mimics the grounds, a series of terraces that wrap into the house.

In the east/west arm of the boomerang, living spaces, accessible through the glazed garden wall, are arranged in a stepped sequence of open rooms: a vestibule with a cast-concrete, built-in bench with a storage slot for shoes; a living room; then a mezzanine dining/kitchen area. A small passageway connects these rooms to the children's bedrooms and bathrooms in the back. At the kitchen level, overlooking the living room, a narrow "bridge" flips back along the north wall, which is lined with shelves for the owners' extensive library, and connects the children's wing to their parents' floating offices and bedroom suite. The north/south arm of the structure is also conceived as a bridge, held aloft by slender steel columns and a utility room; the resulting breezeway doubles as a carport and entryway. Outside, steel fins installed like angled blinkers next to windows facing the street seem merely decorative—details derived from palm fronds—until the architect explains that they shield an overscaled school building from sight and direct the eye toward bay views.

Unlike many modernists, Saitowitz is not fetishistic about new materials, finding them a distraction he avoids assiduously. Simple materials—stucco on the exterior and formaldehyde-free plywood, plasterboard, and nontoxic paint inside—are juxtaposed against one luxury, a living room floor of sustainable mahogany the owners love. These are combined to construct a space that is novel in shape but not just for the sake of invention. It is suited to the owners' casual lifestyle, tied indelibly to its site, and shaped by forces that acknowledge one neighbor's view, sun exposure for another, and open space for the neighborhood.

After all, "the essential medium of architecture is space: a void to be filled with life," Saitowitz says. "I am more interested in what buildings give forth . . . what they allow."

LEFT Exterior deck stairs are designed as extensions of steps within the interior, a fully glazed wall forming a discreet boundary between the two. The wall lets in the south light to supplement radiant heating throughout. FACING PAGE A flight of stairs leads to the couple's bedroom and separate offices. The mezzanine landing is designed as an informal reading lounge.

## STAUB WEEKEND COMPOUND
### A RANCH NEAR THE RUSSIAN RIVER

Hawaii is never far away at Sweetwater Ranch, which covers over 240 acres in the mountains near Guerneville, just above the Russian River. On their ridge overlooking the river valley, Judith Flanders, a psychoanalyst, and James Staub, an investment banker, decided to build a family vacation compound in the spirit of the island homes of Hana, the isolated town at the east end of Maui. It would be a place for their now-scattered brood to gather on weekends, and appropriately, they turned the design over to their son Jonathan, a San Francisco–based interior designer and the family spokesman.

"We are of Hawaiian descent on my mother's side," explains the younger Staub, also an entrepre-

neur like his Scottish grandfather, to whom he bears a closer resemblance. "I grew up in Hawaii. This is as far east as I have ever lived."

At first, Jonathan Staub, an avid remodeler himself, envisioned an arts and crafts–style bungalow like the Maybecks he used to admire during the years his large family spent together at Hawthorne Terrace in Berkeley. Working with Guerneville architect Dirck Bass, Staub helped to design a large structure that was within the area's building codes, but still not large enough to accomodate parents, siblings, cousins, and grandchildren.

The plan did not feel right; it was not the hacienda or compound model they wanted so much. "We

wanted to spread out so we could engage with the land," Staub says. Their intent to have a structure that was diffused to minimize the visual impact on the site seemed to have failed. Then, quite by chance, a solution emerged when Staub and other family members mulled the idea of pitching tent cabins on raised platforms as temporary shelter during construction, rather than sleeping in trailers.

"We threw away our old drawings and decided to keep the tents permanently, and surround the main building with them," says Staub. Bass designed a couple of simple wood-frame pavilions clad with stained cement boards, with pitched shed roofs that overhang deep porches. One is Flanders' private sanctuary, while the larger of the two is shared by everyone.

The tents were set up along the ridge, using wood frames, real doors and windows, galvanized brackets, and polycanvas skins that can last up to five years. "You can get a plan and build your own," says Staub, who has since gone into business with the tent manufacturer. Nestled among the live oaks, they disappear from view until dusk, when their lantern glow becomes mesmerizing, linking the living spaces in the main house with individual bedrooms.

Each "room" has antiques, flea-market finds, and personal memorabilia to give it an *Out of Africa* look that Staub enjoys. His own tent is fitted with windows originally used in buildings within the San Francisco Presidio, and mosquito netting covers his canopied bed. Two guest tents installed near the house are the only ones supplied with electricity.

ABOVE A view from Jonathan Staub's favorite meadow overlooking the ranch house. FACING PAGE A cinder block fireplace and chimney for the living space doubles as an outdoor fireplace that warms the terrace. In the distance, a lap pool and poolhouse.

Even the wood-frame pavilion used by the whole family has a tentlike quality inside, with an armature of wood beams criss-crossed overhead like parts of a Buckminster Fuller geodesic dome, while the translucent hand-troweled plaster walls recall stretched fabric. A metal ladder leads up to a reading loft suspended over a long dining table (from the Old Yosemite Hotel in Petaluma, circa 1890) placed near library shelves. A baronial fireplace and islands of furniture imported from Bali and Hawaii define informal living spaces in the open, loftlike space.

A large open kitchen and a professional chef's pantry are clues to the younger Staub's other big passion: food. Built on a north-south axis, the main house has large roll-away mahogany doors at each end that open to views of the valley on one side and to a trapezoidal lap pool on the other. The seamless stained-concrete floors flow uninterrupted from the

FACING PAGE Tin roofing covers an outdoor wood-and-stucco shower for two. THIS PAGE At night, Staub's inviting Bungalow's tents become beacons in the unlit landscape.

porch into the interior of the house, further blurring the line between indoors and outdoors. A poolhouse built parallel to the pool contains an open shower stall and a steam room.

In the garden, planned by Gary Ratway, herbs are planted and later gathered by friends who visit on "work weekends." Although there will be more-organized plantings, such as fruit-bearing olives, Staub wants the garden to have a natural look. In a kind of Hawaiian gesture to honor the land, they are planting a wild meadow instead of a lawn. "We even planted some flowering weeds … nine hundred of them," says Staub gleefully.

FACING PAGE & ABOVE In clement weather, barn doors on tracks roll back; troweled concrete floors throughout make the transition from inside to outside seamless. The kitchen island is wainscoted. A ladder leads up to a play loft for the children. RIGHT Inside, Staub's tent is remarkably like the main pavilion with its exposed beams. Antiques and flea-market finds are recycled in this modern-day pioneers' camp.

# A PRIVATE PIED-À-TERRE

## A HIGH-RISE APARTMENT ON RUSSIAN HILL

A proponent of vernacular modernism in the Bay Area, the late and noted architect William Turnbull was famous for country houses so well integrated into their sites that the gardens become extensions of enclosed living spaces. His rooms, such as those in the seminal structures some hundred miles north of San Francisco Bay at Sea Ranch, designed in association with Charles Moore and Joseph Esherick, often open to the outdoors. When a couple, executives in the banking business for whom Turnbull had designed a suburban house nearly two decades earlier, asked William Turnbull Associates to design a sizable pied-à-terre in a 1960s International Style high-rise on San Francisco's Russian Hill, the firm welcomed the opportunity to connect outdoor and indoor space in a city setting. Eric Haesloop at Turnbull's office (now called Turnbull Griffin & Haesloop) was the project architect for the first city apartment in the firm's long and impressive history.

The thirty-four hundred-square-foot apartment on the fourteenth floor has prime views: San Francisco Bay and the downtown area.

"We decided to create circular volumes within this rigid rectilinear box," says Haesloop. The typical plan in most of the building's apartments—small rooms off

FACING PAGE The living space is conceived as a landscape, with the dining room a promontory from which to take in the view. Sculpture of a female figure by Manuel Neri; painting on bookcase by Louis Gugliemi. ABOVE Storage spaces—the owners were prepared with linear foot requirements—were dovetailed within the wall systems to be completely invisible; wall panels opens to reveal a television set or a bar. RIGHT From the entry, a view of Mt. Tamalpais.

either side of a central corridor—was eliminated entirely, except for essential structural elements and a circular column housing the pipes and ducts that run from the bottom to the top of the building.

Aiming to enhance and incorporate the three-sided wraparound view, Haesloop devised the dining room as an elliptical domed "promontory" that juts toward the north view. Mullion windows were replaced with floor-to-ceiling sheets of glass for unobstructed views on all sides of the space. "The ceilings were oppressively low," says Haesloop, a problem that was resolved by vaulting ceilings to form a sort of curved roofline. Living spaces have been broadly opened to be free flowing, but with pocketed partitions that can be drawn to shield the bedroom or the kitchen from view. The curved walls and ceilings are sheathed in warm wood, with

accents of cherry wood and insets of sumptuous suede leather by Jacques Quisquater, who crafted the interiors. The anigre veneer for the sumptuous paneling came from a single tree, meticulously apportioned to cover all the required surfaces. "We literally used our last panel to cover the dishwasher," Haesloop says.

FACING PAGE The bathroom is tiled with a lilac-colored mosaic similar to that chosen by Turnbull for the couple's earlier suburban home. A frosted-glass panel slides over clear glass to provide privacy in the generously scaled bath. The ceiling is aluminum leafed.

THIS PAGE The kitchen, above, has every conceivable modern amenity, all organized in a small space. The dining room divides public and private spaces. Sliding panels open the master bedroom to the dining room, an unusual arrangement the couple prefers for their time alone in their city pied-à-terre. The domed dining room ceiling is leafed in aluminum, a reflective sky. What seems like a curved panel around the ceiling canopy is actually carefully fitted facets. The dining table, custom-made by Ross Craig, expands to seat twelve in a circle. Throughout, vaulted maple ceilings conceal recessed lighting strips, a maze of beams, and utility pipes.

A PAINTING THAT IS ITS O

JUNE 19, 1968. IDEA CONCE
NATIONAL CITY CALIF. BY
JULY 30. CANVAS BUILT A
JULY 31. TEXT PREPARED
AUGUST 1. PAINTING COM
UGUST 3. PAINTING C
CTOBER 6. FIRST SHC
ARNES GALLERY, LO

NOTE
FOR EACH SUBSEQUENT
THIS PAINTING, ADD DA
ELOW, FOR EXTRA SP
ADDITIONAL CANVAS

ROOM FOR HISTORY

## DIAZ-AZCUY RESIDENCE
### AN APARTMENT ON RUSSIAN HILL

Interior designer Orlando Diaz-Azcuy is not an obvious modernist. "Futuristic solutions are not my thing," he declares. However, Diaz-Azcuy—also a trained architect and a former design principal with Gensler & Associates—is familiar with modernist clarity. In his pristine San Francisco flat in a 1913 beaux arts building on Russian Hill, he has deftly combined neoclassical antiques with contemporary art, giving formality a fresh, modern face.

In his home, his collection of things is presented in an uncluttered fashion. "I want to show a relation of time," he says, "but one can appreciate the past and also be contemporary." Pooling his resources as a modern architect and an aficionado of antiques, he is now what he calls a designer of restraint. "I like quality and complexity in the finishes, and I always respect good architecture and respond to it," he says. In a sense, that has been the battle cry of many regional modernists as they respond to the conditions of a site, vernacular building idioms, and the Bay Area climate.

In Diaz-Azcuy's flat, the bare, ebony-stained floors, the crisp white living room walls, and a hushed, darkened, silk-upholstered library are simple studies in blacks, whites, and grays. These elements in part were planned to highlight the elegantly proportioned rooms and to create uncomplicated

FACING PAGE In the living room, *Sisters*, a 1992 painting by Lordan Bunch, contrasts with Louis XVI–style mirrors and Neapolitan neoclassical chairs; French grisaille scenic wallpaper is framed like poster art in the dining room. A plaster molding of interlocking rectangles dresses up white walls in the vestibule. ABOVE Vases, arranged atop a green commode in the manner of the mid-twentieth-century painter Giorgio Morandi, complement an ever-changing view of Alcatraz.

backdrops for his collection of antiques, French grisaille panels, and contemporary paintings.

"I like to simplify a room's design so you can look at things and appreciate what's there," says the Cuban-born designer. "But there's always room for baroque flamboyance."

THIS PAGE An uncomplicated palette of whites, blacks, and grays in ebony-stained hardwood floors, pale walls, and white lacquered ceilings throughout the apartment acts as a counterpoint to the darkened postmodern library. FACING PAGE "I wanted the library to be a night room, for reading," Diaz-Azcuy says. Its walls are upholstered in deep green silk. A mottled, painterly ceiling framed in gilt molding is by Juliet Klass. Columned bookcases hold a pair of eighteenth-century Italian pedimented frames and late-nineteenth-century neoclassical urns. In the hallway is a 1974 oil, *Atlantis*, by Jerry Buchanan.

# CRISMAN/BROCK RESIDENCE
## A CONDOMINIUM NEAR BUENA VISTA

Richard Crisman, head of advertising for The Gap company's Old Navy division, and Jeff Brock, an investor, lived right next door to the 1920s Edwardian condominium they wanted in San Francisco's park-like Buena Vista neighborhood. The two-bedroom apartment with its own garden was exactly right for them, and when the previous owner, interior designer Stephen Brady, decided to sell, they were the first to know.

The space they inherited had a very different kind of interior—one given to miscellaneous antiques and collectibles and shabby chic furniture—than what Crisman and Brock envisioned. Wall paneling was stained dark, and the fireplaces had old-fashioned wood mantels. French windows looked onto a classical, tiered garden with boxwood and garden statuary.

Aiming for an uncluttered, modern, clean-lined space to complement their small collection of photographs and lithographs, Crisman and Brock decided to work with colorist James Goodman to lighten the palette. The dark paneled walls were bleached and whitewashed throughout. The old fireplace in the dining room was left intact, but was stripped and painted; the mirrors on either side of it, installed by the previous owner, were also left in place. A stained-glass window

FACING PAGE The new Liagre dining table with its X base became a pivotal piece in the interior, informing Karen Nicks's selections for other rooms; the chairs are from the Holly Hunt collection. ABOVE In the hall, a Matteo Grassi bench of wengé wood and leather webbing, from Limn, below a framed J. John Priola photograph. Mirrors flanking the old-fashioned fireplace double the dining area visually. RIGHT The minimalist wood-paneled living room is whitewashed.

near the breakfast nook was replaced with frosted glass. New cabinets around the living room fireplace were designed to replicate existing 1920s features, and the mantel was reclad using French limestone.

A taupe, black, and white palette is the prevailing motif throughout the remodeled interior. The monochromatic mood is soothing in the manner of a great reading room, with comfortable seating and very few distractions or visual noise.

Instead of working with an interior designer who might not have understood the look they were after, Crisman chose Karen Nicks, a stylist he had worked with on photo shoots, to be a partner in the design. "She helped put everything together," he says, setting off the simplicity of the space with furniture inspired by, or actually from, the 1930s.

"Although I like older architecture," Nicks says, "I suggested a break from it to make a space that was a mixture of modern and old. I like antiques from the 1930s."

She introduced the owners to furniture by the French designer Christian Liagre, which is designed with restraint and a modernist clarity of line. The first piece they acquired, a dining table of wengé, an African hardwood, convinced the owners to get similar furniture in every room. Some pieces of furniture were either custom-built to suit the Liagre originals or antiques, such as coffee tables from the 1930s in the living room. Liagre-style sofas are covered in wool felt—appropriate in the winter and even during San Francisco's foggy summers—and grouped around the antiques. They face the garden, which still shows signs of work done by the previous owner.

"They wanted to move toward a more Japanese aesthetic with fewer things out on display than they used to have," says Nicks.

For the bedroom, Nicks designed an armoire, made by Tom Sellers of San Francisco, that recalls the look of a Japanese tansu chest. The mismatched bedside tables, paired with a custom bed of maple, are all Liagre originals. Alongside the windows, a chaise made by Fitzgerald is covered in a comfortable, textured fabric called Teddy.

The spare room doubles as an office where Crisman has a cupboardful of stationery stacked in meticulous piles. "I like order and having everything in its place. I function better that way," he says.

"There is a time constraint working with Richard and Jeff because they are both busy travelers. A lot of European furniture has to be ordered months ahead of time. Even the Manuel Canovas fabric took six months to be delivered," says Nicks. "The custom pieces were easier to work with because sometimes you need to tweak things a bit, and that's not as easy when the pieces come from a great distance."

Casual entertainers, the pair wanted the apartment to be comfortable and stylish enough either to slouch in or to have a cocktail party at short notice. "That's why we spent a lot of time picking the right things," says Crisman.

The beautiful light coming into the apartment is kind to Crisman's small collection of artwork, which includes silver-print photographs by J. John Priola and Diane Arbus. These hang on walls in the living room and bedroom, and Richard Diebenkorn lithographs, in the dining room.

The garden is still a tiered hodgepodge with neoclassical statuary that will be changed over time. Meanwhile, says Crisman, "I like the contrast between inside and outside."

"I'm not attached to things. But there's a line between minimalism and simplicity," says Crisman. "Still, people who come over often ask when we are going to be finished."

FACING PAGE In the bedroom, Nicks's tansu-style armoire design works well with a simple custom bed of maple flanked by mismatched Liagre bedside tables. A Diane Arbus print hangs above the fabric-covered chaise. THIS PAGE In the living room, the old fireplace is modernized with a French limestone fascia; it contrasts stylishly with new built-in shelves and cabinets deliberately designed to match older period details. In the kitchen, cabinet doors were replaced with simple painted versions that modernize the room without having to take the old but efficient cabinetry apart. A breakfast nook looks out onto the garden.

## SIEDLER RESIDENCE
### A REMODELED HOUSE ON RUSSIAN HILL

Dan Siedler's remodeled 1927 house on Russian Hill—barely seventy years old but considered architecturally significant in the city register—seems like a synopsis of Bay Area building history leading up to present-day modernism.

When Siedler, a young radiologist, acquired it a few years ago, it was still a two-level craftsman-style house built in the tradition of Bernard Maybeck, but in great disrepair. It was ivy-covered, with a facade worth saving but ruined on the inside. The bulk of the house had been stripped away to form two apartments; the roof leaked; and the undeveloped basement was a rodent maze. A small view of the bay, charming front balconies, a little enclosed porch, and one beautiful room with dark wood paneling and original fireplace tiles showing farmers and field animals were enough, however, to lure Siedler into a two-year-long renovation journey.

Siedler chose Daren Joy of North American Stijl Life to return the interior to some semblance of its original form and to create a three-level addition in the back that respected the turn-of-the-century sensibility without slavishly repeating typical embellishments of the era.

Joy phased the project, first remaking the original shell, then building the addition in the back. He divided the interior spaces with a minimum of walls and built-in furniture, and avoided space-wasting hallways, creating consonant volumes to echo the proportions of the three original rooms in the front, which were left

FACING PAGE In Siedler's craftsman-style house, the new living room ceiling is beamed; a black-and-white brush painting hanging near a round dining table of rolled steel and copper is by Sandy Walker. TOP A view of the unchanged facade and the three-story addition. ABOVE Dark wood built-in cabinets salvaged from a school have metal and plywood shelving by Park Furniture.

THIS PAGE Copper cladding around the fireplace bounces off wavelike reflections above the hearth. "Since Siedler is a radiologist, we liked the idea of using a shielding material in the house," says architect Daren Joy. For all its still beauty, metaphor, and careful detailing—such as a glass and wood pocket door to the bedroom, above—Joy's overall design is principally functional. The desk in the bedroom tilts shut when not in use; the windows pivot. A Mexican retablo of an operating-table scene, set within the desk alcove, is one of many such images Siedler has found for his collection in the basement "grotto." The chair is by Thonet. FACING PAGE A pivoting window in the all-tile bath is paned, using pressed glass salvaged from antique windows and washboards. The steel and concrete sink top is custom-made. The master bedroom has wood beams to echo the original rooms on the lower floor, but has an updated, galvanized metal ceiling. A modern brush painting by Sandy Walker hangs above the bed; the bedside table is a Russel Wright original. The door to the balcony is also salvaged.

mostly intact. "There was nice detailing and we left it. I like modernism, but I also like some feeling and texture," says Joy. A new stairway leads to the master bedroom on the top floor, and another goes to the basement where Siedler has a garden-level workshop for craft projects.

"During the process I learned so much about architecture and quality of space that my ideas changed dramatically. I began to appreciate the freedom that uncluttered space provides," says Siedler, looking on the bright side of having to camp within bare, loftlike interiors stripped down to plywood floors during construction. Enjoying the new perspectives the open plan allowed, Siedler opted for a sculptural kitchen with no walls. It is designed as a freestanding cube defined by counters built on a square plan, with floor-to-ceiling storage towers at each corner. Throughout the

house, the extensive and simple use of cold-rolled steel, cast concrete, aluminum-stained wood, and copper paneling, as well as furnishings from the 1960s and 1970s, add modern notes.

"Our approach was not to try to recapture lost history, but to create an ambiguity of time and style," says Siedler. This was achieved in the upstairs of the all-new wing, for example, by using craft materials such as wood beams, copper, tile, and salvaged vintage glass with modernist detailing—like a cantilevered roof overhang and a pocket door of wood and glass. Hand-crafted stairs with industrial-style steel railings—ubiquitous in loft spaces—hardly seem incongruous in this polished update.

FACING PAGE The tall storage towers in the open-to-view kitchen, of aluminum-stained birch, stand alongside countertops of stained concrete. A chair on the landing, a Scandanavian antique, is by Jens Risom. BELOW A copper-clad wall "shields" the addition from the original wing of the house. RIGHT In this kitchen, the chef has the best views.

BAY REGION INTERNATIONAL

## BISCHOFF RESIDENCE
### A HOUSE IN THE OAKLAND HILLS

Like so many others who lost beautiful, even historic homes by Bay Area architects of note in the 1991 Oakland Hills fire, artist Adelie Bischoff lost hers. Even though the fire took her things—a collection of prehistoric beads, art by friends such as Richard Diebenkorn, her own paintings, and nearly a thousand of her husband Elmer Bischoff's drawings—her greatest loss happened a year earlier, when Elmer died.

"Elmer and I had never considered building a house, and I didn't think I wanted to rebuild *here*," she says. "Elmer had died, and when I walked out of that house—just in time, they tell me—I really let go of it," says Bischoff.

Barely two days later, however, in a rented, skylit, multilevel loft space with a large studio on the ground floor, she experienced an epiphany. "I was always trying to make our old Berkeley contemporary home look like a Maybeck, with wood and stained glass, and suddenly, to my great surprise, I was in this modern mode," Bischoff says.

Joseph Slusky, a friend and sculptor whose work she displays abundantly in her new home, introduced Bischoff to San Francisco architect Stanley Saitowitz. "I saw a model of his Holocaust memorial for Boston, and I said to him, 'It's your baby.'"

Bischoff wanted to wait a year before getting the house started, so she could create new paintings for a show. "But Stanley told me that planning a house was a very creative process, and it would help my painting. He was right," she recalls.

Saitowitz visited the two-and-a-half-story loft she was staying in and surely must have responded to her enjoyment of it. "It was like a nest, and I have that here," she says, looking around the three-thousand-square-foot space that now envelops her.

FACING PAGE A cast-concrete fireplace, gypsum walls, maple floors and cabinetry, and steel give Adelie Bischoff's East Bay aerie an International Style edge. Modern classics such as Alvar Aalto bar stools reinforce the high modern notes. "I went to the stores with her. She let me have an educating role," says architect Saitowitz. The idea of the house as a gallery was important to Bischoff anyway; she likes to display her own satirical comments on capitalism—images of shoes, running feet, stockinged legs—alongside work by her late husband, Elmer Bischoff. THIS PAGE Arne Jacobsen chairs in the dining room; living room chair by Frank Gehry.

The lot is one of the smallest in the area, below par by current standards, so the architect planned the house with no outside space except for a shallow deck facing bay views. "It's an urban plan," Saitowitz admits. "It's not an object house, and we

built the interior instead. The facade is merely an expression of the inside. It's not really a facade— the interior planes are being pushed through the box," says the architect. The most challenging aspect of the design was to respond to the topography, allowing the house to cascade down the hill. "When you get inside the front door, people's mouths drop open as the space falls away," Saitowitz says.

Two structural steel frames, painted gray-green and set within the center of the house, free the space from the constraints of load-bearing walls and partitions. When you cross the threshold at the front door, you stand on a landing that overlooks the living areas below. What Bischoff, a gregarious woman who likes having people to the house, now has is a space she can command at a glance. It is like old Roman houses with a central courtyard. "I didn't think that would be possible on a sloping site," she says.

Large windows are open to wide views that dense but now burned-away pine and eucalyptus woods had shielded from sight for decades. Portions of rooms—the kitchen, the dining room, and a passage leading to Bischoff's large, fifteen-by-forty-eight-foot painting studio on the same level—are also visible from the entry landing, creating a sense of transparency and layering not commonly found in live/work lofts. "It's natural when you design for one person," says Saitowitz. "You only need to be in one space at any one time." By keeping the different spaces transparent but separate, Saitowitz has achieved a spatial complexity with myriad views. "It's intimate, but you can be a voyeur with people on the stairs and in the studio."

## BECKER RESIDENCE
### A HOUSE AND STUDIO IN THE OAKLAND HILLS

"I saw thick smoke from the deck as I was talking on a portable phone," remembers graphic designer Leslie Becker. "I'm a pessimist. I took my handbag and some Polaroids and fled. The house burned down maybe half an hour later."

For Becker, as for many others who lost their homes in the devastating 1991 Oakland Hills fire, the experience was traumatic, but starting over in the same area was important to her.

A former architecture student, she briefly thought that this might be her chance to design her own house, "but that idea lasted for exactly thirty seconds," she laughs. Becker did not want to repeat her old house, whose design was burned into her memory. "I had what my son Jason would describe as 'muscle memory' in the way I navigated my old house. I could never have seen it differently."

Instead, she dropped a note in architect Jim Jennings's mailbox at the arts college where they both teach, asking if he would design her new place. Becker laid down her requirements—a protected deck, a place to take in the views, extra bedrooms for visiting children, a garage and a studio space for her work—and then left the design process alone. "This wasn't about authorship and ego," says Jennings. The architect and the designer were both aware that any design takes on its own life, one that needs to evolve

LEFT  From the street, Becker's split structure has two separate facades: the house clad in Eterboard, the garage in aluminum.
ABOVE  A screen of frosted glass between the facades blocks out the rest of the house, which steps down the site. Small cubist structures when viewed from the street, the wings of Becker's house stretch inward to envelop twenty-two hundred square feet of space.

uninterrupted. The old house was conventional: a single floor, with a predictable deck hugging the width of the bayside wall—a feature that many of the new homes on the hill have repeated—and without protection from the frequently high winds that buffet the hills. The design Jennings created was unlike anything Becker could have imagined, although it was exactly in tune with her preference for modernist design. "I stared at the model in wonderment. I had it on an ottoman in front of me as I waded through insurance papers. It induced me to go on," says Becker.

To open the house to the sun and views and yet shield it from the wind, Jennings designed two buildings that enclose an open space between them. The

LEFT Inside the home, the living room has anodized aluminum details and a floor made of jara wood. The stairs that lead to bedrooms below are of the same wood.
ABOVE A model of the house shows the rear at a glance.
FACING PAGE A steel-and-wood deck with bay views spans the space between house and garage/studio. The bedrooms have access to a yard down a wood staircase.

design seems merely utilitarian, until a longer look reveals remarkable details.

Toward the back, where the views are, a broad bridgeway that spans the open space between the buildings also serves as a deck. "The open spaces aren't obvious. My deck feels like my stoop in New York. It's private," says Becker. Using the downward-sloping site to advantage, Jennings borrowed loosely from a house the Swiss modernist Mario Botta designed in Italy. Each building has an entry "ramp" stacked over a U-shaped structure built on the site.

"By digging the house in just a couple of feet, we gained a story in elevation," says Jennings, proud of his distribution of the twenty-two hundred square feet of built space. The illusion is of a bigger, roomier house that leaves plenty of open space on the small lot. The ramp to the left contains a kitchen in the front section that connects seamlessly with the living room that overlooks the hills. The ramp to the right contains a two-car tandem garage that rests above the spare bedrooms on the lower floor. To emphasize the functions of each structure, the architect clad one in fire-resistant cement Eterboard and the other with corrugated aluminum sheeting.

"There isn't an obvious window wall like so many of the new structures around here have. There are views *through* the house," says Becker. Reflections in the anodized aluminum and glass doors and windows to the deck continue the horizon line, subtly suggesting a broader view.

Translucence also plays a part. A wall of reinforced frosted glass between the two buildings shields the open spaces between them but creates an illusion of openness. A staircase that leads from the

living room to the bedrooms below also has a wall of frosted glass. "The closer you come to it, the more transparent it gets," says Jennings, "and as you move away, the image beyond the wall becomes obscure." This versatile glass wall rises from the master bedroom floor and is pinned into the opening of the living room floor above, where it cantilevers upward to form the guardrail for the stairs. As a wall, it creates privacy, but it also becomes a poetic point of light. "This way, the lower bedroom has access to light that isn't obvious," says the architect.

Even the rooms have an ambiguous quality. Bedrooms are suggested, but they easily convert to

ABOVE A carefully detailed kitchen is made roomier by pushing out storage units into exterior bays, their faces flush with interior walls. LEFT A frosted-glass wall cantilevers upward from the bedroom floor to become a guardrail upstairs. RIGHT It lets light into the master bedroom below, but its obscured surface allows privacy.

studios or a study, their built-in closets invisible behind walls. The back section of the garage serves as Becker's home office and studio.

In true modernist tradition, the palette is subdued, the colors pointing clearly to the materials themselves. A gray/green ceiling is complemented by the natural reddish brown of the polished jara, an Australian wood used for floors in the living room and stairs to the bedroom. Silvery anodized aluminum sheeting surrounds the fireplace, almost blending in with the white walls. Subtle details enhance the illusion of space and movement within this strictly cubist envelope. For example, a one-inch groove between the walls and the eleven-foot ceilings makes the ceiling seem like it is floating. Ebonized oak storage units for the kitchen are pushed into wall openings so that they are flush with the wall surface, adding space within the small room; the cabinet backs project as anodized aluminum–clad bays on the outside. Narrow horizontal slit windows above the cabinets bring in light and also emphasize the openings from within. "It's a way of creating a larger scale to the space," says Jennings.

Two spare bedrooms and two bathrooms complete the lower U-plan. The inner courtyard, just off the bedrooms, is actually a wood terrace with wide steps leading down to a concrete retaining slab and a tiny back garden of black slate and shrubs. The stairs double as seats for Becker's open-air gatherings.

Bereft of her old possessions and collections, Becker sees her house as a metaphor for dispassionate modernism that awaits a softening touch: "This house has an absence of history ... but I'll fill it slowly."

## JOHNSON/BATES RESIDENCE
### A HOUSE IN ST. HELENA, NAPA VALLEY

At first glance, when you drive up to the promontory where Los Angeles–based architect Scott Johnson's second home sits, high in the Mayacamas Mountains above St. Helena in the wine country, all you see is a series of "shoe boxes" on end, grouped together playfully—an elementary lesson in modernism—and painted primary red, yellow, and blue.

The deliberate opacity of the design as seen from the driveway is a careful maneuver to gain privacy for a young family that is much in the limelight in its homeland in Southern California. Johnson's wife, Dr. Meg Bates, did the first in-vitro fertilization in San Diego and is Madonna's obstetrician and a target of the tabloids. Johnson, whose firm Johnson Fain Partners has been responsible for high-profile projects such as Fox Plaza in Los Angeles, developments in south Asia, and—right in the wine country—Opus One Winery, has to be available for calls from around the world. Johnson and Bates's house in Los Angeles is so different, so urban, that it was important for them to experience the outdoors completely in their setting among the vineyards above St. Helena. "It took the children three days to get used to the idea that it was all right to go out and play," Johnson jokes.

The forty-six-year-old architect says that when he travels, he carries his wine country house in his head, both as a beacon of refuge and as an object lesson for the work he does. Many of his firm's corporate projects, Opus One for instance, lean toward eclectic, even historicist designs, so it is surprising to learn that his own taste leans toward modernism. Johnson's approach, however, is derived from a more benign California tradition of domestic architecture such as that espoused by masters such as Rudolph Schindler, the Bay Area's Joseph Esherick, and artist Donald Judd, whose asymmetrical masterpieces Johnson also holds in high esteem.

Deconstructing classicism to reveal durable tenets of design has been the ruling impetus of Johnson's private musings on architecture. "I don't like angry modernism," he laughs. Like many architects, Johnson has designed numerous pieces of furniture derived from classical models and simplified them to suit his modern taste. Many of these prototypes are scattered within the interior of his house, which does not immediately reveal its own classical conceits.

LEFT A surprisingly classical, transparent southeast elevation takes in views. Exterior materials—flagstone, cedar siding, and plywood—appear inside as well. ABOVE The subdued east side blends in with the landscape. RIGHT Rough cedar planks clad Scott Johnson's seemingly impenetrable cubist building among vines, where a low stone wall marks the entry.

The house is divided into two zones by a cedar wall that starts outside, flanking the entryway, and cuts all the way through to the southeast-facing living room at the far end, forming a spine for the structure. The eastern section of the house contains the public areas—living, dining, and kitchen areas, as well as a den; the western part contains bedrooms for the couple and their two children and boxy, perfectly square guest rooms with large windows facing westward views of hills. The private, southeast elevation—

invisible from the public road—is exposed on three sides, overlooking a swimming pool perched on the edge of the hill.

A flagstone path leads past the cedar spine into the house, forming a series of levels that emulate the sloping site and step toward the living room at the far end. The passage from outside into the interior becomes a seamless, ceremonial procession, such as can be found in many Pompeiian temples.

"I like bone structures rather than pierced or draped forms," says Johnson. Inside the house, exposed ceilings dissected by long skylights reveal beams that evoke modern lofts, and smoothly finished raw plywood contrasts with rough-sawn cladding to echo the exterior treatment of the building. This reflects lessons learned from Esherick in Berkeley, and a practice that even Wurster encouraged.

"The smallest detail matters," Johnson intones, as though speaking to his class at the University of Southern California. Cinder block, wood, plaster walls, rolled-steel windows, cabinetry of stained-ash veneers, and a suspended silver-leaf ceiling in the dining room come together in surprisingly complex, yet seemingly casual harmony. These are details that might be lost on most observers, but they amuse Johnson endlessly. "I don't like temporary aesthetics," he says, "and I hope to be here a long time."

FACING PAGE In the living room, classic seats by Mies van der Rohe and chairs by Le Corbusier are matched with a couch covered in brocade and a coffee table designed by Johnson.
THIS PAGE Tall steel windows reveal a slice of the surrounding countryside. A chair prototype designed by Johnson, visible past the open door to the master bedroom, was derived from a fifteenth-century Savonarola original. The skylit master bath is tiled with glass mosaic.

## ABERCROMBIE/VIEYRA RESIDENCE
### A HOUSE IN SONOMA

New Yorkers Stanley Abercrombie and Paul Vieyra purchased their place in the California sun ten years before they actually built on the small wine country lot in Sonoma. "We've both been scheming this for quite a while," says Abercrombie, the longtime editor of *Interior Design* magazine and author of several books on architecture and design. Both Abercrombie and Vieyra are also architects, so the design of their dream house became a consuming challenge.

"It was not easy to build on the site," says Abercrombie. One idea, to build two towers with a room in each and a circulation area bridging them, would have saved every tree on the lot, but with code requirements for exits, they decided the structure would have been "too lumpy" with stairs.

The scale of the low single-story, two-bedroom house they ultimately built was determined in part to protect the trees but also by the septic system they needed to install in the rocky ground, as well as by other factors. The great number of books Abercrombie had collected over his long tenure as editor of the magazine had to be housed. "It wasn't just the space," he says. "You don't want to display them and

make them too big in the place." Also, to face the views of the valley, the house had to be oriented toward the northwest, making skylights imperative to bring in good light from the south.

Limited by their budget, Abercrombie and Vieyra designed what seems at first encounter like a stucco-clad symmetrical bunker hunkered down among the live oaks on a downward-sloping ridge site. A red chimney in the center resembles a periscope. The building has a long rectilinear plan, with the entrance in the middle at one level; a galley kitchen, breakfast nook, and office to the left; and a study to the right. Stairs directly opposite the front door step down into an open plan living/dining space flanked at the ends by bedrooms. The northwest wall is fully glazed to pull in the view. The lucid, functional layout recalls the idealistic utilitarian aesthetic of the early modernists. A friend, viewing the house for the first time, quipped, "It's the first Miesian adobe I've ever seen!"

Open to new materials, Abercrombie and Vieyra readily accepted their builder Jacques Mathieu's suggestion to use Ener-Grid, a quake-resistant construction system of ten-foot-long blocks prefabricated with recycled polystyrene and Portland cement that Mathieu's company, MaTerre International, had devised. Foam is used as a form to make a structural grid of concrete with six-inch cylinders horizontally and vertically fifteen inches apart. The foam later serves as insulation when the

ABOVE Abercrombie and Vieyra's Miesian "adobe" is made from a unique foam-and-poured-concrete material called Ener-Grid by MaTerre International. LEFT Two 1935 Breuer Isokon chairs in the living room are from New York, from when Abercrombie first worked for Breuer. FACING PAGE In the study, an Eames lounge chair and ottoman are arranged over a rug from Morocco. On the wall, tribal art from Brazil.

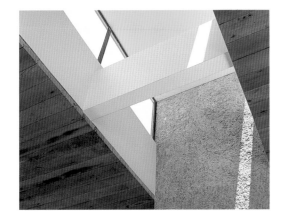

FACING PAGE In the bedrooms at each end of the house, bookshelf walls conceal pocket doors. The headboard (detail above) is upholstered with silk; all closet doors are Formica. RIGHT In the living space, skylights (detail at top) are designed to control direct sunlight. Breuer's cantilevered chrome chairs are a 1928 design from ICF, with cushion upholstery from Rodolph. Atari lamp by Noguchi. Aluminum perforated tiles clad the fireplace wall to add a machined counterpoint to the interior. The sofa, by Weiman/Warren Lloyd is covered with leather.

construction is finished with wood, stucco, or concrete. "We would never have been able to use so much glass without the material's insulation properties," says Abercrombie. For the exterior of their house, what seems like adobe is actually a mixture of cement and earth blown onto the foam and concrete blocks. With four inches of blown material inside and out, the walls are a full eighteen inches thick. "This is a reassuring house to live in, especially in an area where fires are such a problem," says Abercrombie. "A frame house would have cost less, but if you're going to live in a house for a long time, you have to be

sure it doesn't bore you. It's fair to say that this is slightly more expressive than a conventional house."

Inside, bookcases—large wood boxes stacked—are scaled to make the books quieter and more subordinate to the (also robust) architecture. During construction, the owners decided that their palette was getting too earthy—the blown earth/concrete on the walls, the ceiling clad in tongue-and-groove wood recycled from a waterfront warehouse in Oakland, and poured concrete floors—so they opted to "industrialize" the fascia

of the fireplace using a sheet-metal veneer. Redwood terraces beyond the glazed wall, where the owners have a wheeled tent pavilion for outdoor dining, step down to a lap pool at the edge of the site.

"This is similar to a beach house we did in Long Island," says Vieyra, recalling the indoor/outdoor nature of that design, "but this time it's in the mountains."

"One of the things we do miss from the East Coast are old friends," says Abercrombie. "Fortunately, this is a place they are happy to visit."

ABOVE The breakfast table is an old drafting table, a memento of Vieyra's work at Skidmore Owings and Merrill. LEFT The concrete-top round dining table was fabricated by David Jensen, who also poured the floors. The dining chairs are by Mario Botta. Lithographs by Robert Rauschenberg. FACING PAGE The deck— its canopy on wheels—steps down to the pool (detail this page).

# SWATT RESIDENCE
## A HOUSE IN LAFAYETTE, CONTRA COSTA

Several years ago, when San Francisco–based architect Robert Swatt decided to build a home for himself, his wife, Christina (an interior designer), and their two children on land he owned in Lafayette, just east of the Oakland Hills, he incorporated the lessons learned during two decades of living and designing for usually mild California weather.

Their one-and-a-half-acre down-sloping site overlooks a creek and a picturesque oak thicket fringing the hills of Briones Regional Park. To frame the rural views to the north, as well as to draw in the south light, Swatt conceived a sequence of spaces: A guest house (used as an office) incorporates a carport at the street level. A flight of stairs and a ramp bridge lead to the front door of the freestanding Z-shaped house in the middle of the site. Halfway down the hill, the house runs east to west and opens visually and literally on the north and south sides. A swimming pool on the lower, flattest part of the site and a series of redwood terraces are also designed as outdoor rooms, synchronizing with the topography.

The interior is organized around a glazed, south-facing two-story spine that incorporates stairs and passageways lit by skylights and pierced by five folding glass doors that open onto an entry courtyard. When the doors are open, the gravel-covered courtyard becomes an extension of the living spaces within, a device popularized in the tract houses built by developer Joseph Eichler during the 1950s.

The clean, sculptural, colliding rectilinear volumes of the building, the way it anchors to the hill, and the modernist pedigree of the design echo the works of

FACING PAGE In the living room, a japonesque couch designed by Swatt is complemented by contemporary furniture from Limn. RIGHT Hard terrazzo floors are contrasted with wood.

both Rudolph Schindler and a lesser-known California architect, Gordon Drake, whose work from the 1950s Swatt had long admired. Schindler's indebtedness to another Viennese, Adolf Loos—whose rooms explored space rather than aiming for a specific shape or sculptural form—and his fascination with Frank Lloyd Wright's ideas of a connection of the building to the landscape, are also clearly evident in Swatt's interpretation. "I grew up in Southern California around buildings by Schindler and Wright," Swatt says. "The courtyard is a japonesque aspect of the structure … all these ideas come to play. These are the roots of modern California architecture."

Viewed from the north elevation, Swatt's building, with its transparency, cantilevering planes, and terraced decks, is obviously inspired by Schindler's 1929 Wolfe House in Avalon, on Catalina Island.

THIS PAGE The house is split by a spine running east/west. Family areas— the kitchen, living room, and gravel-covered courtyard—have southern exposure, while the formal, public spaces are on the north side where the views are.

FACING PAGE Upstairs, the master bedroom has its private terrace overlooking the pool and the regional park beyond.

Like Schindler, Swatt designed built-in pieces of furniture within the structure—a couch in the living room and banquettes in the kitchen—that are related to the architecture through proportional and formal similarities. For example, the living room couch is a platform built of glue-laminated beams turned horizontally, inspired by a temporary bridge that was used around the site during construction. "The idea kept germinating, and it became furniture. It looks like part of the building—an outdoor slab bench with seats on it," says Swatt. "The bench cantilevers on each side to form tables."

Using terrazzo on the floor in the living spaces (a common material in Christina's native Venezuela) and warmer oak in the bedrooms upstairs, Swatt kept materials and colors relatively simple within the interiors. He used different woods for variation: "hemlock-fir" beams on the ceiling, mahogany for the windows, cedar on the soffits that merge with the exterior, and red-stained birch for cabinets and a built-in bench in the kitchen.

The structural expression of the building on the exterior is also a clue to its internal organization. Horizontal cedar-board siding and mitered glass enclose the central spine, delineating it from the colored-stucco skin of the main living spaces. Formal public spaces face the north views, while family areas and the kitchen surround the courtyard. As a result, "Sunday mornings are on the south side," says Swatt. "We enjoy its vertical and horizontal openness," he says, pointing out that there are virtually no doors at the ground floor—just level changes. "This house does not fit any suburban models," he says, pleased. "It is an attempt to reach an indoor/outdoor California ideal."

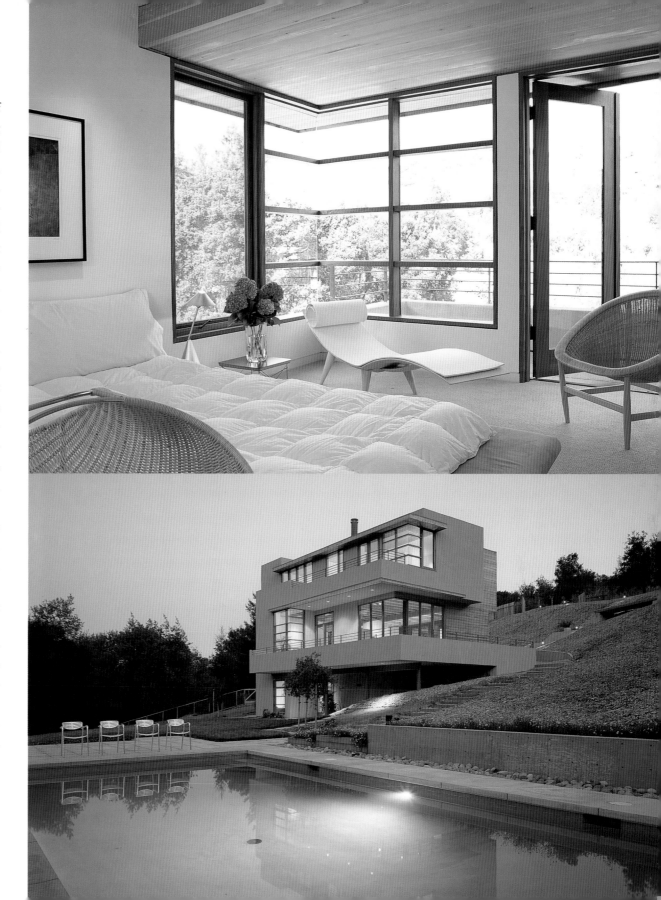

Metal, glass, and wood: Becker house.

## METAL

**Frank C. Borrmann Steel Company**
700 Indiana Street
San Francisco, CA 94107
(415) 621-3063
A versatile source for sheet metal as well as rods and tubes.

**Bayshore Metals Inc.**
244 Napoleon Street
San Francisco, CA 94124
(415) 647-7981
For all types of sheet metal and miscellaneous metal building materials.

**Alco Iron & Metal Company**
1091 Doolittle Drive.
San Leandro, CA 94527
(510) 562-1107
An amazing treasure trove of new and scrap metal parts for creative projects.

**Coast Aluminum**
687 Sandoval Way
Hayward, CA 94544
(510) 441-6600
Sheets and tubing as well as re-cyled cast aluminum.

**Flynn & Enslow**
1530 17th Street
San Francisco, CA 94107
(415) 863-5340
Fabulous metal meshes of different gauges and strengths for screens and dividers. Can be used as diffusers as well.

**Esco Corporation**
30640 San Clemente Street
Hayward, CA 94544
(510) 429-0100
A wholesale resource where you'll need a business license.

**Standard Sheet Metal & Marine Plumbing**
366 Brannan Street
San Francisco, CA 94107
(415) 392-6463
A fair-sized metal shop where the convivial atmosphere makes you feel you've entered a specialty boutique. Superb service.

## GLASS

**Paige Glass Company**
1531 Mission Street
San Francisco, CA 94110
(415) 621-5266
All kinds of laminated and reinforced glass and mirrors.

**Metropolitan Glass Corporation**
3201 3rd Street
San Francisco, CA 94124
(415) 647-5111
For laminated glass in many different colors.

**John Lewis Glass Studio**
10229 Parmain Street
Oakland, CA 94603
(510) 635-4607/08
A source for high-end custom cast glass. His work appears in wall friezes, door panels, or as vases in residences and offices.

## PLASTICS & OTHER LAMINATES

**Tap Plastics**
157 South Van Ness
San Francisco, CA 94103
(415) 864-7360
For Plexiglas, laminates, resins.

**Commercial Plastics**
3241 Keller Street
Santa Clara, CA 95054
(800) 325-1262
Fiberglass sheeting and various plastics and laminates.

**E. B. Bradley Company**
26250 Corporate Avenue
Hayward, CA 94544
(510) 887-4144
An invaluable source for a variety of creative Formica panel designs.

## LUMBER

**Beronio Lumber**
2525 Marin Street
San Francisco, CA 94124
(415) 824-4300
Quality veneers, plywoods, and lumber, with a full-service shop.

**Truitt & White Lumber Co.**
642 Hearst Avenue
Berkeley, CA 94714
(510) 841-0511
A wide range of lumber, including hardwoods and parallel-strand lumber to order.

**Eco Timber International**
1020 Heinz Avenue
Berkeley, CA 94710
(510) 549-3000
Sustainably harvested exotic hardwoods and unusual varieties of woods from around the world.

**Plywood & Lumber Sales**
2035 Newcomb Avenue
San Francisco, CA 94124
(415) 648-7257
PALS, as they like to be called, offers a big inventory of hard-to-find plywoods and hardwoods.

## CONCRETE

**Buddy Rhodes Studio**
2130 Oakdale Avenue
San Francisco, CA 94124
(415) 357-4000
A good source for pre-cast tile, cement counters, and furniture in a variety of colors and textures.

Ted Boerner's *Little Dipper* sofa

## STORES
### SAN FRANCISCO

**Ann Sacks Tile & Stone**
San Francisco Design Center
2 Henry Adams Street
San Francisco, CA 94103
(415) 252-5889
Handcrafted tiles plus stone cut in many sizes. Limited editions and revivals of classic designs suited for modern interiors as well as exterior veneers.

**Arch**
407 Jackson Street
San Francisco, CA 94111
(415) 433-2724
Architect Susan Colliver's colorful graphic store sells supplies for designers, architects and artists in an imaginative contemporary setting. Papers, frames, pencils, and one-of-a-kind objects.

**Britex Fabrics**
146 Geary Street
San Francisco, CA 94108
(415) 392-2910
The most complete one-stop shop for a range of fabrics for upholstery ranging from wool to vinyl.

**Builders Booksource**
900 North Point
San Francisco, CA 94109
(415) 440-5773
Practical books on building materials, architecture, interior design, and gardens.

**MAC**
5 Claude Lane
San Francisco, CA 94108
(415) 837-0615
Housewares and furnishings.

**Clervi Marble Company**
221 Bayshore Boulevard
San Francisco, CA 94124
(415) 648-7165
A purveyor of quality stone for eighty years; marble, granite, onyx, travertine and limestone countertops, vanities, fascias and pedestals have been its mainstay.

**Decorum**
1400 Vallejo Street
San Francisco, CA 94109
(415) 474-6886
Restored deco, moderne and occasionally modern lighting.

**De Vera**
384 Hayes Street
San Francisco, CA 94102
(415) 861-8480
580 Sutter Street
San Francisco, CA 94102
(415) 989-0988
and 29 Maiden Lane
San Francisco, CA 94108
(415) 788-0828
Modernist objects displayed among casual finds ranging from antiques such as collectible glass from the 1950s to furniture by Donald Judd to contemporary artworks, home accessories, and exotic handmade jewelry. Original furniture, glass, and accessories by Federico de Vera.

**F. Dorian**
388 Hayes Street
San Francisco, CA 94102
(415) 861-3191
Contemporary accessories.

**Fillamento**
2185 Fillmore Street
San Francisco, CA 94113
(415) 931-2224
A pioneering store on a thriving block, Iris Fuller's store has been the anchor for a neighborhood revival during the last fifteen years that has made this part of Fillmore a shopping experience. Modern derivatives and unusual lamps, linens, beds, furniture, and accessories abound in this three-level store filled with ideas.

**Flax Art & Design**
1699 Market Street
San Francisco, CA 94103
(415) 552-2355
Art books, papers, lighting, furnishings, accessories, and supplies for framing and art projects can be found in this store or in their exhaustive catalog.

**Gump's**
135 Post Street
San Francisco, CA 94108
(415) 982-1616
Although the store has built its reputation since 1861 as a trove of Asian ware, art, and accessories, its newly revamped line orchestrated by Geraldine Stutz includes subtle contemporary wood and glass crafts. Included are art pieces by woodworker Ed Moulthrop and Italian glass master Lino Tagliapietri, and other timeless furnishings.

**Highlights**
105 Valencia Street
San Francisco, CA 94103
(415) 575-1230
Excellent European lighting.

**ICF Group**
550 Pacific Avenue
San Francisco, CA 94133
(415) 433-3231
A brand-new retail store for modernist furniture traditionally sold only to the trade. Many classics among new designs.

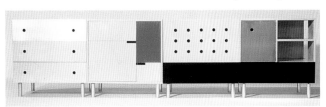

CCD Designs' *City Block* storage designed by Christopher Deam at Limn Company.

**Japonesque**
824 Montgomery Street
San Francisco, CA 94133
(415) 391-8860
Barely a few doors away from Bill Stout's bookstore specializing in architecture, Koichi Hara's collection of graphics, sculpture, glass, and furniture highlights Japanese design principles also espoused by the modernists—harmony, simplicity, and the use of humble, unembellished materials.

**Limn Company**
290 Townsend Street
San Francisco, CA 94107
(415) 543-5466
A super-store filled to the brim with contemporary furniture and lighting by every major manufacturer in the United States as well as Europe, including limited editions by local tal-

ent. This is the place to shop for works by Le Corbusier, Ray and Charles Eames, Jens Risom, or Carlo Molino. Contemporary art shows and events at Limn's gallery often showcase works by local architects and designers.

**Macy's**
170 O'Farrell Street
San Francisco, CA 94102
(415) 397-3333
The furniture section, the decorative accessories department, and the cellar are sometimes a source for contemporary design.

**Pottery Barn**
2100 Chestnut Street
San Francisco, CA 94123
(415) 441-1787
The San Francisco–based company owned by Williams-Sonoma has stores citywide and in different locations all over the West. As their catalog selections demonstrate, this vibrant company aims for an affordable, pleasing "soft" modern style.

**Richard Hilkert Bookseller**
333 Hayes Street
San Francisco, CA 94102
(415) 863-3339
Long a friend of the fine printing world, Richard is the ultimate source for out-of-print design books as well as the latest editions on a variety of subjects.

**Rizzoli Books**
117 Post Street
San Francisco, CA 94108
(415) 984-0225
This impressive, downtown bookstore rivals others specializing in books on design, architecture, and photography.

**San Francisco Design Center**
2 Henry Adams Street
San Francisco, CA 94103
(415) 490-5800
Long the stronghold of design professionals, this incredible resource for contemporary furniture now welcomes retail customers willing to work with in-house designers in hundreds of showrooms: Agnes Bourne, Randolph & Hein, Kneedler Fauchere, Palacek, Donghia, Enid Ford, Houles, and others.

**San Francisco MuseumStore**
151 Third Street
San Francisco, CA 94103
(415) 357-4035
The first museum on the West Coast devoted to twentieth-century art now has an extraordinary store that stocks new furniture and product designs (often included in the museum's permanent collection) as well as books on art, architecture, and media art.

**Waterworks**
235 Kansas Street
San Francisco, CA 94103
(415) 431-7160
Bath fixtures, tile, and stone.

**William Stout Architectural Books**
804 Montgomery Street
San Francisco, CA 94133
(415) 391-6757
Architect Bill Stout has probably built more design libraries up and down the West Coast than buildings. His store in the Jackson Square area specializes in basic and hard-to-find architecture publications, especially on twentieth-century design.

**Zinc Details**
1905 Fillmore Street
San Francisco, CA 94115
(415) 776-2100
Furniture and home accessories
designed by architects and
craftspeople as well as reissues of
Eames chairs and other classics
displayed in a witty setting.

BERKELEY

**Berkeley Mills**
2830 Seventh Street
Berkeley, CA 94710
(510) 549-2854
Japanese- and Mission-influ-
enced furniture built to order to
suit contemporary homes.

**Builders Booksource**
1817 Fourth Street
Berkeley, CA 94710
(510) 845-6874
Design and architecture books,
as well as a source for books on
gardening and building.

**The Gardener**
1836 Fourth Street
Berkeley, CA 94710
(510) 548-4545
Alta Tingle pioneered a store
inspired by her love of gardens
long before gardening became
trendy. Sculptural boulders,
tools, vases, and furniture are
chosen for originality and clean,
simple design.

**Lighting Studio**
1808 Fourth Street
Berkeley, CA 94710
(510) 843-3468
Contemporary lamps and
lighting design services.

**The Magazine**
1823 Eastshore Highway
Berkeley, CA 94710
(510) 549-2796
Rainer Lagemann's two-story
red barnhouse of a store is filled
with most of the classics of modern furniture: pieces by Le Corbusier, Eileen Gray, Aalto, Rietveld, and Eames are displayed
alongside contemporary European creations from Artemide,
Kartell, Aero, Cappellini, and
Italiana Luce. Garden furniture
is displayed *in situ* in Rainer's
well-designed garden.

**Urban Ore**
1333 Sixth Street
Berkeley, CA 94710
(510) 559-4455
Look for what you can't find
elsewhere at this salvage yard
full of furniture and fixtures.

SAUSALITO

**Heath Ceramics, Inc.**
400 Gate 5 Road
Sausalito, CA 94965
(415) 332-3732
Veteran sculptor Edith Heath
creates colorful ceramics—tiles
for indoor and outdoor use as
well as shapely dinnerware—in
the Bauhaus aesthetic she has
espoused since the fifties.

MILL VALLEY

**Smith & Hawken**
35 Corte Madera Avenue
Mill Valley, CA 94941
(415) 381-1800
The flagship nursery and garden
store caters to every style imag-
inable, but is particularly atten-

tive to modern tastes. Also in
San Francisco, Berkeley, Palo
Alto, Los Gatos, and Santa Rosa.

SAN ANSELMO

**Modern I**
500 Red Hill Avenue
San Anselmo, CA 94960
(415) 456-3960
Steven Cabella specializes in
modern, mid-century furnishings from the thirties to the
sixties. Classic vintage furnishings, furniture by architects, ob-
jets, and artwork are all at home
in this modernist building.

ST. HELENA

**Ira Wolk Gallery**
1235 Main Street
St. Helena, CA 94574
(707) 963-8800
Contemporary paintings.

PALO ALTO

**Crate and Barrel**
530 Stanford Center
Palo Alto, CA 94304
(415) 321-7800
At this latest store—among
many Bay Area versions of this
national chain— a selection of
modernist furniture is also available alongside stylish kitchen-
ware.

**Polo/Ralph Lauren**
650 Stanford Shopping Center
Palo Alto, CA 94304
(650) 326-1710
A sort of rugged, contemporary
elegance pervades Ralph Lauren's selection of furniture and
housewares.

BIBLIOGRAPHY

*A Matter of Taste:
Willis Polk's Writings on
Architecture in* The Wave
Edited by Richard W.
Longstreth
1979, The Book Club of
California, San Francisco

*An Everday Modernism:
The Houses of William Wurster*
1995, The Museum of Modern
Art, San Francisco
University of California Press,
Berkeley

*Architecture in California:
1868-1968*
David Gebhard and Harriette
Von Breton
1968, The University of
California, Santa Barbara

*Architecture in North America
Since 1960*
Alexander Tzonis, Liane
Lefaivre, Richard Diamond
1995, Thames and Hudson
Ltd., London/ Little, Brown
and Company, Boston

*Frank Lloyd Wright, Architect*
1994, The Museum of Modern
Art, New York

*History of Modern Architecture*
Leonardo Benevolo
1977, MIT Press, Cambridge

*Interior Design of the 20th Century*
Anne Massey
1990, Thames and Hudson
Ltd., London

*Inventing Kindergarten*
1997, Norman Brosterman
Harry N. Abrams, Inc.,
New York

*Landmarks of Twentieth-Century
Design: An Illustrated Handbook*
Kathryn B. Hiesinger and
George H. Marcus
1993, Abbeville Press,
New York

*Minimum*
John Pawson
1996, Phaidon Press Limited,
London

*Modernism*
Richard Weston
1996, Phaidon Press Limited,
London

*Old Forms On a New Land:
California Architecture in
Perspective*
Harold Kirker
1991, Roberts Rinehart,
Niwot, Colorado

*On The Edge of The World:
Four Architects in San Francisco
at the Turn of the Century*
Richard Longstreth
1983, The Architectural History
Foundation/MIT Press,
Cambridge, Massachusetts

*R.M. Schindler:
Composition and Construction*
Edited by Lionel March and
Judith Sheine
1993, Academy Editions/
St. Martin's Press, New York

*San Francisco Architecture*
1992, Sally Woodbridge,
John M. Woodbridge
Chronicle Books, San Francisco

*Understanding Modern
Architecture*
George Barford
1986, Davis Publications,
Worcester, Massachusetts

*Additional photo credits:*
*Pages 12-13: Cowell House photographs, courtesy of Mr. and Mrs. Harry Parker III*
*Page 14: Drawing by Bernard Maybeck, courtesy of the College of Environmental Design, University of California, Berkeley*
*Page 16: Photographs courtesy of the Roger Sturtevant Collection, The Oakland Museum*
*Page 17: Photographs courtesy of Ernest Braun*
*Page 18: Photograph courtesy of George Homsey / Esherick, Homsey, Dodge and Davis*